75 200X
D1138168

LEISURE AND CULTURE
DUNDEE

C00675200X

| | |
|---|---|
| Bertrams | 11/09/2012 |
| | £7.99 |
| DGLAS | 567.9 |

SCHOLASTIC discover more™

# dinosaurs

By Penelope Arlon
and Tory Gordon-Harris

# How to discover more

*Dinosaurs* is packed with prehistoric creatures and filled with great facts about them. By knowing a little bit about the way the book works, you will have fun reading, and discover more.

## Dino adventure

The book travels through time to introduce the great dinosaurs of the Triassic, Jurassic, and Cretaceous periods. Learn about fossils, fossil hunters, and amazing dinosaur record setters along the way.

*The introduction sets up the big fight scene.*

*The caption tells you about* Stegosaurus' *opponent,* Allosaurus.

*The fact box tells what each dinosaur ate, shows how HUGE it was, and lots more.*

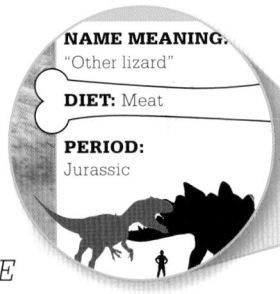

# Digital companion book

Download your free all-new digital book,

## Dinosaur Face-Offs

**Log on to**
**www.scholastic.com/discovermore**

**Enter your unique code:**
**RCN4MM3P6K3D**

**Watch six fierce dinosaur fights**

Small words describe the action and give bite-size facts.

The timeline across the top shows when the dinosaurs lived.

Look up a favourite subject in the contents.

Learn how to say dinosaurs' names, and look up or learn new words in the glossary.

The labels tell you which dinosaur is which.

**Find out more**

This takes you to another page to learn about other related facts.

Look up a word in the index and find which page it's on.

The words along the bottom are questions or amazing facts.

**Click the pop-ups for facts and stats**

**Encyclopedia entries to discover even more**

**Fun dinosaur quizzes**

**Consultant:** Kim Dennis-Bryan, PhD
**Art Director:** Bryn Walls
**Assistant Designers:** Clare Joyce, Ali Scrivens
**Managing Editor:** Miranda Smith

**Cover Designers:** Neal Cobourne, Natalie Godwin
**DTP:** Sunita Gahir
**Visual Content Editor:** Diane Allford-Trotman
**Executive Director of Photography, Scholastic:** Steve Diamond

Copyright © 2012 by Scholastic Inc.

All rights reserved. Published by Scholastic Inc., *Publishers since 1920.* SCHOLASTIC, SCHOLASTIC DISCOVER MORE™, and associated logos are trademarks and/or registered trademarks of Scholastic Inc.

No part of this publication may be reproduced, stored in a retrieval system, or transmitted in any form or by any means, electronic, mechanical, photocopying, recording, or otherwise, without the written permission of the publisher. For information regarding permission, please write to Scholastic Inc., Attention: Permissions Department, 557 Broadway, New York, NY 10012.

Library of Congress Cataloging-in-Publication Data Available

Distributed in the UK by
Scholastic UK Ltd
Westfield Road
Southam, Warwickshire
England CV47 0RA

ISBN 978 1407 13464 2

10 9 8 7 6 5 4 3 2 1  12 13 14 15 16

Printed in Singapore 46
First edition, September 2012

Scholastic is constantly working to lessen the environmental impact of our manufacturing processes. To view our industry-leading paper procurement policy, visit www.scholastic.com/paperpolicy.

# Contents

**The world of the dinosaurs**

**8** What is a dinosaur?
**10** Hall of fame
**12** Life on Earth
**14** Introducing dinosaurs
**16** More dinosaurs
**18** Dinosaur detectives
**20** Fossil clues
**22** Dinosaur guesswork

**Triassic and Jurassic dinosaurs**

**26** Triassic and Jurassic collection
**28** Other ancient creatures

**30** *Herrerasaurus*
**31** *Coelophysis*
**32** The Bone Wars
**34** Dinosaur eggs
**36** *Diplodocus*
**38** Super-giants
**40** *Compsognathus*
**42** *Stegosaurus* vs *Allosaurus*
**44** Jurassic rock

**Cretaceous dinosaurs**

**48** Cretaceous collection
**50** *Iguanodon*
**51** *Spinosaurus*
**52** *Edmontosaurus*
**54** Amazing skulls
**56** *Velociraptor* vs *Protoceratops*
**58** Gliding dinosaurs
**60** Ankylosaurs
**62** Mighty *T. rex*
**64** A giant discovery!
**66** Digging up Sue
**68** *Triceratops*
**70** End of the dinosaurs
**72** Dinosaurs today
**74** History of discovery
**76** Pronunciation guide
**77** Glossary
**78** Index
**80** Thank you

# The world of the dinosaurs

For 165 million years, Earth belonged to the dinosaurs. Through thick forests and damp swamps, giant meat-eaters like this *T. rex* bellowed and gnashed their ferocious teeth, looking for prey.

# What is a dinosaur?

Dinosaurs were animals that lived millions of years ago. Some were the most colossal creatures ever to have lived on land.

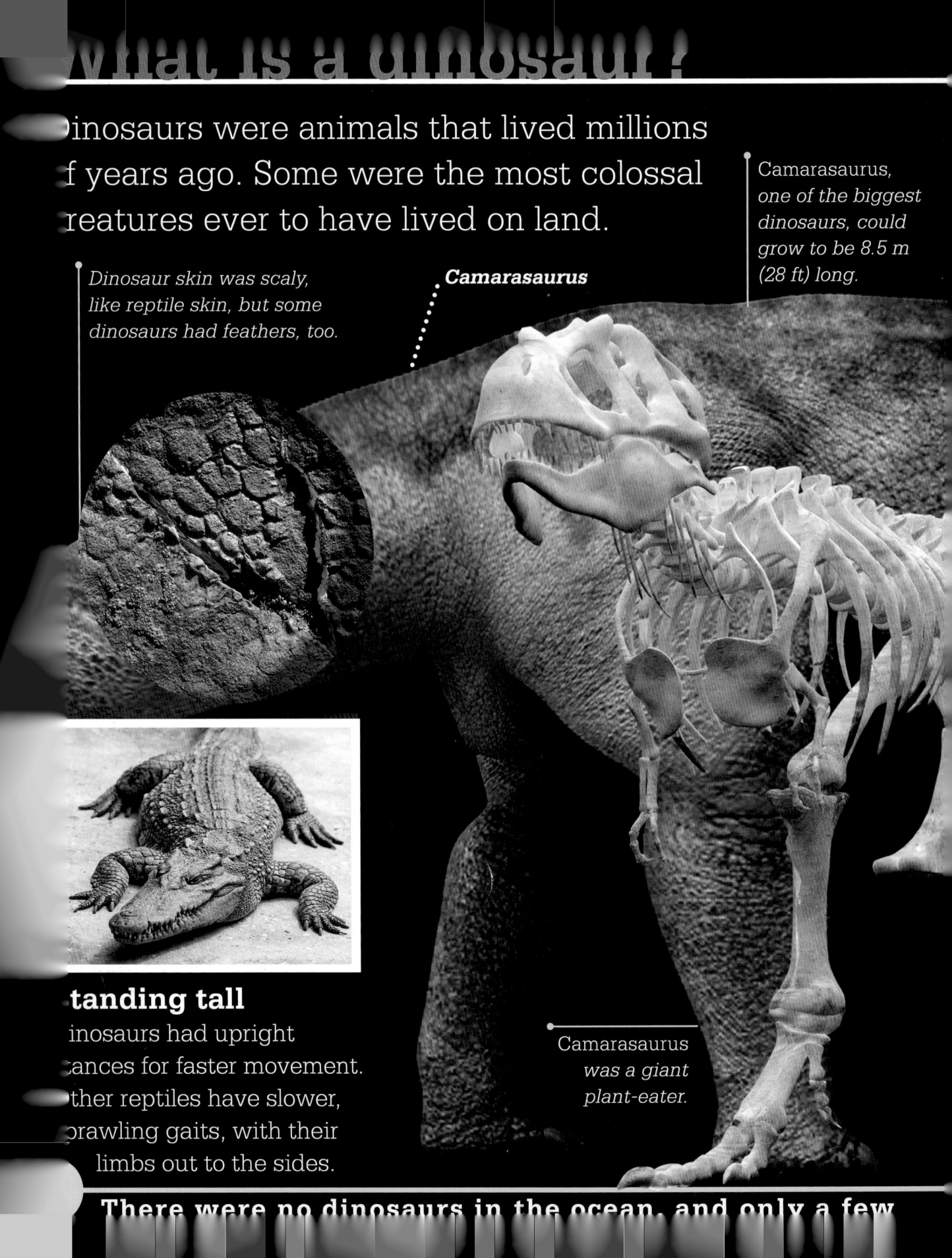


*Dinosaur skin was scaly, like reptile skin, but some dinosaurs had feathers, too.*

Camarasaurus, *one of the biggest dinosaurs, could grow to be 8.5 m (28 ft) long.*

Camarasaurus *was a giant plant-eater.*

## Standing tall

Dinosaurs had upright stances for faster movement. Other reptiles have slower, sprawling gaits, with their limbs out to the sides.

**There were no dinosaurs in the ocean, and only a few**

## How to spot a dinosaur

Dinosaurs all had scaly skin, long tails, teeth, and four limbs. Some walked on two legs, some walked on four, and some walked on either two or four!

## Big and small

The smallest adult dinosaurs known were about the size of today's birds. All dinosaur babies were tiny when they hatched from eggs – this sauropod baby might have grown up to be a *Camarasaurus*!

***T. rex* skeleton**

**human**

*We know what dinosaurs looked like only because we have found their fossilized bones – like these, of a meat-eating* T. rex.

## What colour were dinosaurs?

Nobody knows! Scientists have recently discovered a dinosaur feather's colour, but their skin could have been spotted, striped, or purple!

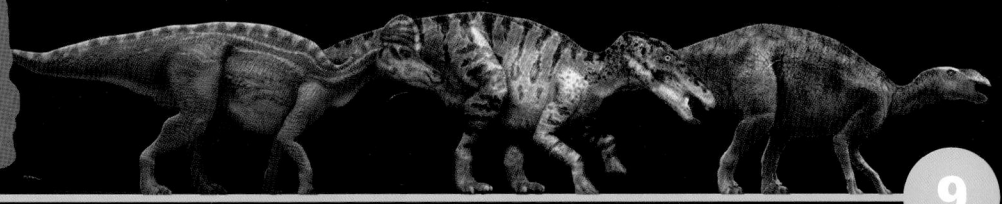

could glide in the air. Dinosaurs lived mainly on land,

# Hall of fame

Dinosaurs were among the most awe-inspiring animals to have lived on Earth, so the record setters of the dinosaur world were truly amazing!

**BIGGEST MEAT-EATER**
Giganotosaurus *was one of the biggest meat-eating dinosaurs. It probably hunted* Argentinosaurus *– what an impressive sight that would have been!*

**FASTEST RUNNER**
*Ostrich-like* Gallimimus *could probably run at a rate of 65 kph (40 mph) – about as fast as a racehorse.*

**BIGGEST SKULL**
Torosaurus *had a huge skull that stretched 2.6 m (8.5 ft) in length.*

**FIRST IN SPACE**
*In 1985, pieces of* Maiasaura *bone and eggshell flew into space on a space shuttle.*

**BIGGEST DINOSAUR**
Argentinosaurus *grew up to 35 m (115 ft) in length. That's as long as five African elephants standing trunk to tail!*

**WEIRDEST-LOOKING**
Therizinosaurus *was a bizarre plant-eating dinosaur with massive claws on the ends of its long arms.*

**MOST TEETH**
*Some of the plant-eating hadrosaurs had up to 1,000 cheek teeth for grinding food in the sides of their jaws.*

**SMARTEST DINO**
Deinonychus *was a speedy, wily dinosaur with a large brain for its body size.*

**SMALLEST DINO**
Microraptor *was one of the smallest dinosaurs. It was the size of a pigeon.*

**BEST ARMOUR**
Ankylosaurus *had super-tough plated skin covered with spikes, and a clubbed tail.*

**. . . had the longest name.**

# Life on Earth

Dinosaurs lived between 230 and 65 million years ago. That's a LONG time ago. Life on Earth is divided into periods of time called eras. This is what was living in the eras before and after the dinosaurs.



**PRECAMBRIAN** 4,600–542 MILLION YEARS AGO

**PALEOZOIC** 542–251 MILLION YEARS AGO

## Precambrian era

Life first appeared on Earth, in the form of tiny living things in water.

*About 350 million years ago, fish with lungs and four limbs first crawled ashore. Life on land began.*

## Paleozoic era

During this era, the first land animals appeared: insects, reptiles, and cynodonts (early mammal-like animals).

**tetrapod**

**dragonfly**

*By the late Paleozoic era, huge reptiles, such as* Dimetrodon, *lived on Earth.*

***Dimetrodon***

## Time of mass extinction

Lots of creatures died out.

TRIASSIC

## Mesozoic era

The dinosaurs appeared during this era. It is divided into three periods: Triassic, Jurassic, and Cretaceous.

**Triassic**
***Coelophysis***

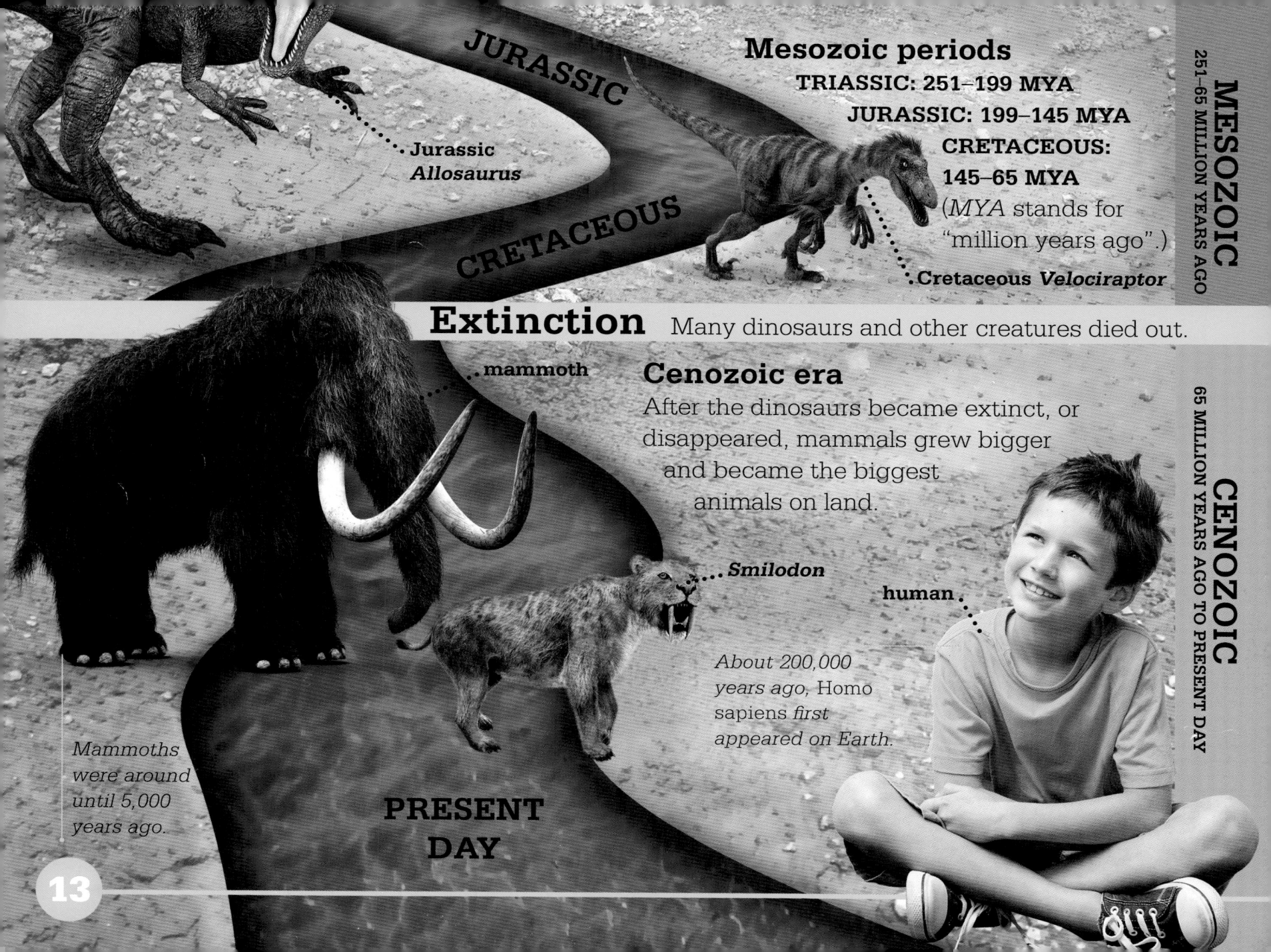


## Mesozoic periods

**TRIASSIC: 251–199 MYA**

**JURASSIC: 199–145 MYA**

**CRETACEOUS: 145–65 MYA**

(*MYA* stands for "million years ago".)

**MESOZOIC**
**251–65 MILLION YEARS AGO**

## Extinction

Many dinosaurs and other creatures died out.

## Cenozoic era

After the dinosaurs became extinct, or disappeared, mammals grew bigger and became the biggest animals on land.

**CENOZOIC**
**65 MILLION YEARS AGO TO PRESENT DAY**

*About 200,000 years ago,* Homo sapiens *first appeared on Earth.*

*Mammoths were around until 5,000 years ago.*

# Introducing dinosaurs

Twelve dinosaurs are shown on the next four pages, from early dinosaurs to the last ones that lived on Earth. Their fossilized remains show us that they existed in all shapes and sizes.

**Find out what these dinosaurs ate, how they lived,**

what they might have fought throughout this book.

# More dinosaurs

As time passed, dinosaurs changed body shapes and found new ways to defend themselves. By 65 million years ago, dinosaurs were in their prime.

**We know of about 540 kinds of dinosaur, but as many**

000 kinds might have lived, or perhaps more

# Dinosaur detectives

Nobody has seen a dinosaur alive – we can only study their fossilized remains. But with a little detective work, fossil experts called paleontologists can find out what dinosaurs looked like, and sometimes how they behaved.

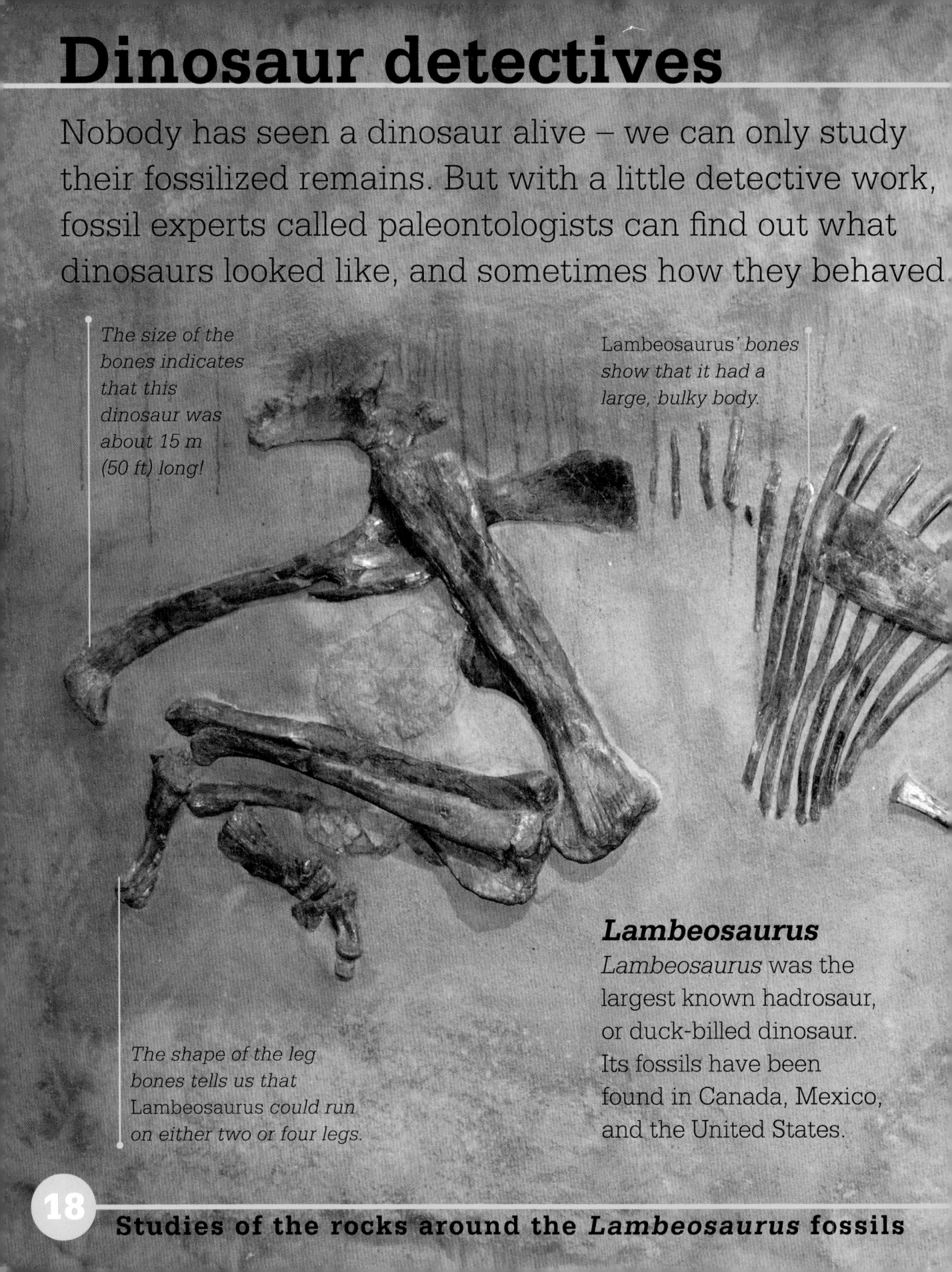

*The size of the bones indicates that this dinosaur was about 15 m (50 ft) long!*

Lambeosaurus' *bones show that it had a large, bulky body.*

*The shape of the leg bones tells us that* Lambeosaurus *could run on either two or four legs.*

### *Lambeosaurus*

*Lambeosaurus* was the largest known hadrosaur, or duck-billed dinosaur. Its fossils have been found in Canada, Mexico, and the United States.



**Studies of the rocks around the *Lambeosaurus* fossils**

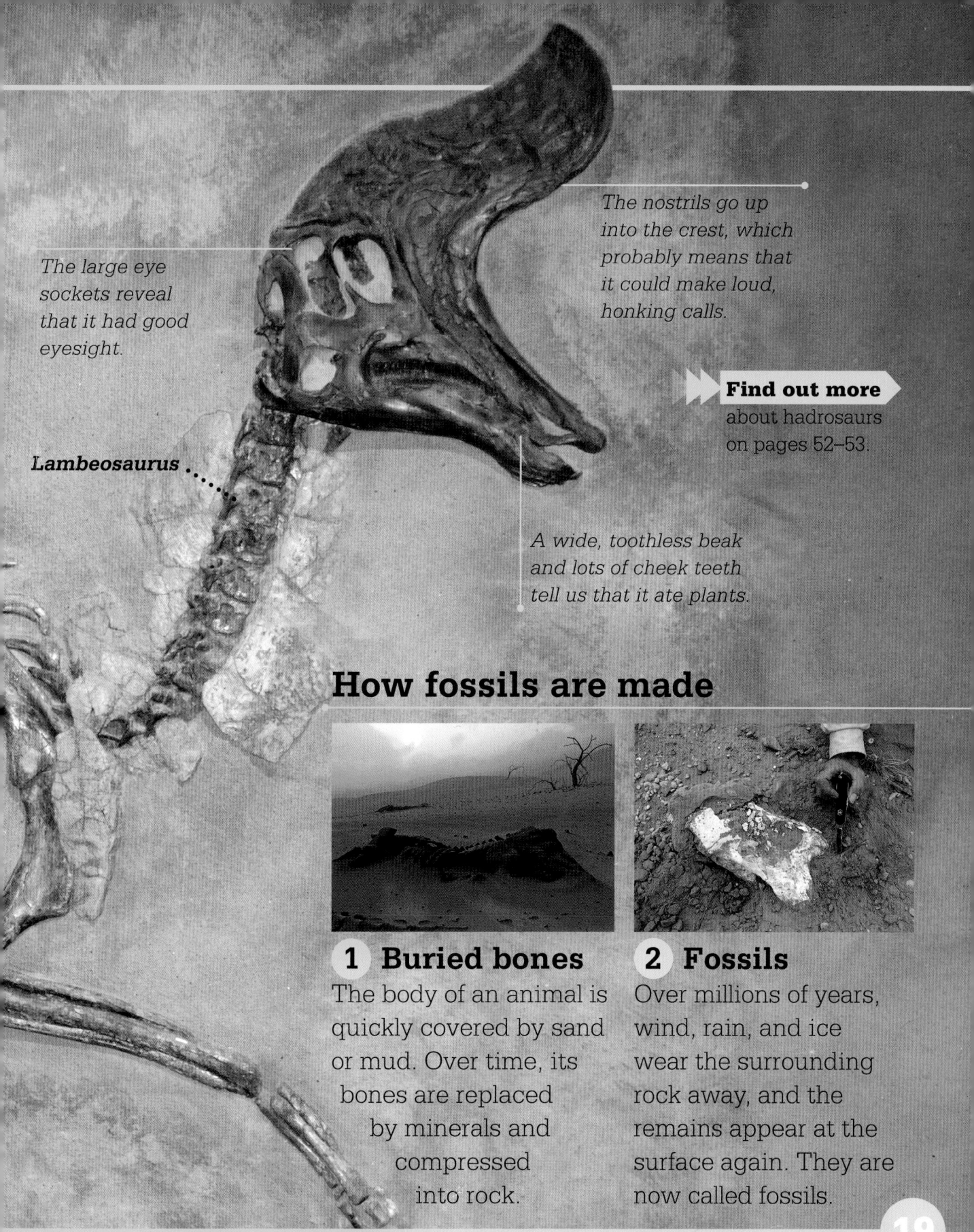


**Find out more** about hadrosaurs on pages 52–53.

## How fossils are made

### 1 Buried bones

The body of an animal is quickly covered by sand or mud. Over time, its bones are replaced by minerals and compressed into rock.

### 2 Fossils

Over millions of years, wind, rain, and ice wear the surrounding rock away, and the remains appear at the surface again. They are now called fossils.

**show that the dinosaur lived in the Cretaceous period.**

# Fossil clues

## Bones

Fossilized bones tell us what a dinosaur looked like, and the surrounding rocks give clues to help paleontologists work out how long ago the dinosaur lived.

## Footprints

The tracks and strides shown in fossilized footprints tell scientists how fast an animal ran, how heavy it was, and if it moved in a group.

## Skin

Only a few examples of dinosaur skin or skin impressions have been found. However, from these fossils, we know that dinosaurs had scaly skin.

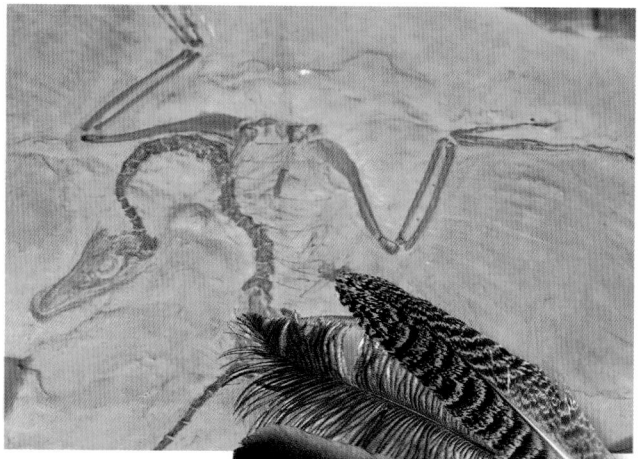

## Feathers

A few fossils have shown that some dinosaurs had feathers on their bodies.

*The feathers were very similar to these bird feathers.*



**New fossil evidence is being found all the time. And**

## Coprolites

A coprolite is fossilized animal poo. Dinosaur coprolites can tell us about the dinosaur's last meal. Dinosaur poo may contain seeds, wood, leaves, fish, or bones.

## Eggs

Fossils prove that dinosaurs laid eggs. Scientists have found fossilized eggs with adult dinosaur fossils, which means that some dinosaur parents looked after their eggs.

## Plants

Fossilized plants found near dinosaur bones give us clues about what plants were growing at the time and therefore what particular dinosaurs may have eaten.

## Animals today

Scientists study animals today to try to explain how dinosaurs might have behaved. This African wild dog hunts in packs, perhaps like many dinosaurs did.

# Dinosaur guesswork

Often only small parts of a dinosaur are discovered, so paleontologists have to work out what the whole dino looked like. There's a lot they disagree on, and much more to find out!

**Lonely skull**

Only the skull of *Pachycephalosaurus* has been found. It has an unusual hard dome on the top.

*Some paleontologists think that males butted one another to fight over females.*

**Picturing a dinosaur**

After comparing *Pachycephalosaurus*' skull with skulls of different dinosaurs, scientists think that it may have had a bulky body, walked on two legs, and used a heavy tail to help it balance.

***Pachycephalosaurus* skull**

***Pachycephalosaurus* illustration, based on the skull and on other dinosaurs**

## *Iguanodon* mystery

When Gideon Mantell dug up *Iguanodon* bones in 1825, the study of dinosaurs was new, so his ideas had mistakes. But in 1834, a more complete *Iguanodon* skeleton was found.

*Mantell thought* Iguanodon *was a mammal-like lizard.*

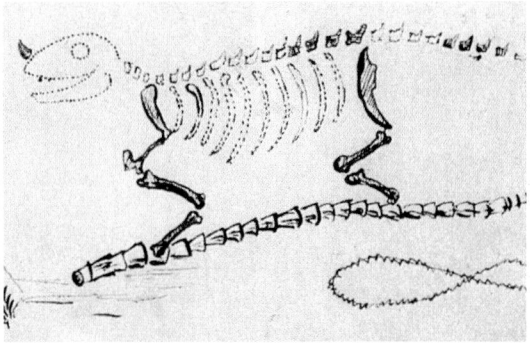

*He thought* Iguanodon*'s spike was on its nose!*

*Now we know it was a dinosaur, with a spike on its thumb.*

# Triassic and Jurassic dinosaurs

Between 230 and 145 million years ago, during the Triassic and Jurassic periods, giant meat-eaters like *Allosaurus* and massive plant-eaters such as *Stegosaurus* clashed in dramatic fights.

# Triassic and Jurassic

The first dinosaurs appeared in the Triassic period. By the end of the Jurassic period, giant meat-eaters and colossal plant-eaters roamed Earth.

Allosaurus
Compsognathus
Shunosaurus
Elaphrosaurus
Kentrosaurus
Plateosaurus
Barapasaurus
Dryosaurus
Eoraptor
Monolophosaurus
Apatosaurus

# Other ancient creatures

No dinosaurs lived in the ocean. But at the same time that dinosaurs roamed the land, huge meat-eating reptiles lurked beneath the waves, and others flew overhead!

## Ocean giants

Reptiles such as *Liopleurodon* grew to be the size of large dinosaurs. They also became extinct at the same time as the dinosaurs did, so none remain in the oceans.



**Giant ocean reptiles are long gone, but some fish and**

## What else lived on land?

Dinosaurs were not the only creatures that lived on land during prehistoric times.

*Giant flying reptiles called pterosaurs flew through the skies, some the size of small aeroplanes.*

*Insects like this dragonfly flew around before, during, and after the time of the dinosaurs.*

*Huge land reptiles hunted the dinosaurs. Some of them were as long as a bus!*

*All of the mammals in the dinosaurs' world were small. Many looked like the rats and shrews of today.*

*Ichthyosaurs looked like fish but were actually reptiles.*

**sea creatures haven't changed much since dinosaur days.**

# Herrerasaurus

TRIASSIC JURASSIC

*Herrerasaurus* is the oldest dinosaur to have been found so far. It lived about 228 million years ago. Its fossils were first found in 1956 by a rancher in South America

*Its long, pointy head had small, sharp teeth for gripping prey.*

**HERRERASAURUS**
**(herr-ray-rah-SORE-us)**

**NAME MEANING:**
"Herrera's lizard"

**PERIOD:**
Triassic

**DIET:** Meat

## Early meat-eater

*Herrerasaurus* was one of the biggest dinosaur hunters of its time. It ran on two legs and had a long tail to help it balance.

## Discovery!

Find a brand-new dinosaur, and it might be named after you! Victorino Herrera was the rancher who first spotted *Herrerasaurus* fossils in Argentina.

**In 1988, the first intact *Herrerasaurus* skull was found**

# Coelophysis



*Coelophysis* was a fast, vicious meat-eating dinosaur of the Triassic period. It was the size of a small car.

## Death in an instant?

Many *Coelophysis* fossils were found together at Ghost Ranch, New Mexico, USA, as if a huge catastrophe, such as a flash flood, killed them all at once.

Coelophysis *had large eyes, which means it had good eyesight for hunting.*

## Look out!

*Coelophysis* was at war with other Triassic reptiles. It could catch smaller ones, but it was hunted by large predators such as phytosaurs, giant crocodile lookalikes that were as long as school buses.

Coelophysis *was fast enough to catch small reptiles.*

**COELOPHYSIS**
**(seel-OH-fie-siss)**

**NAME MEANING:**
"Hollow form"

**PERIOD:**
Triassic

**DIET:** Meat (small reptiles)

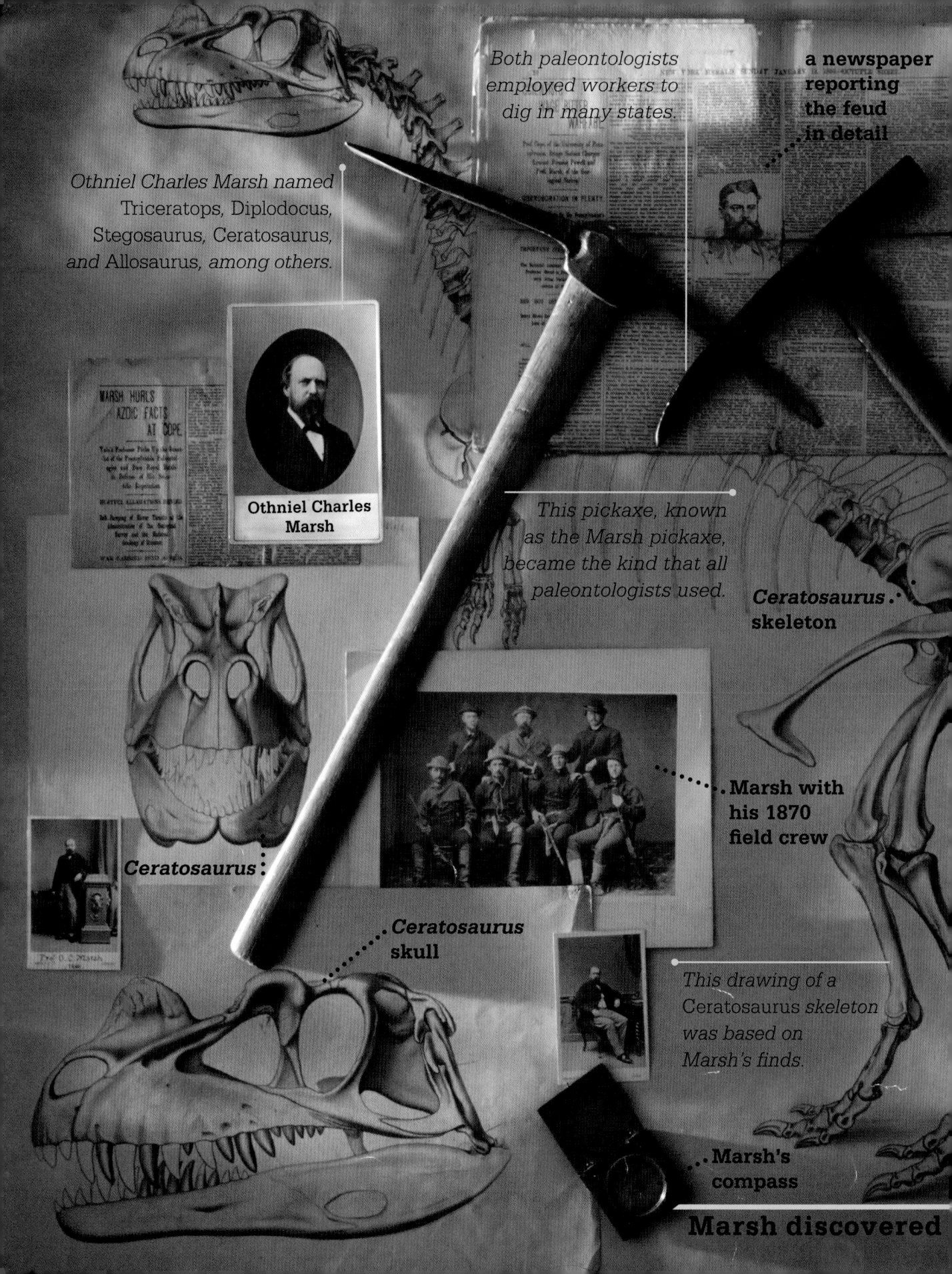


**Marsh discovered**

# The Bone Wars

In the late 1800s, a huge number of dinosaurs were found by two American paleontologists, Marsh and Cope, who aggressively competed to discover the most.

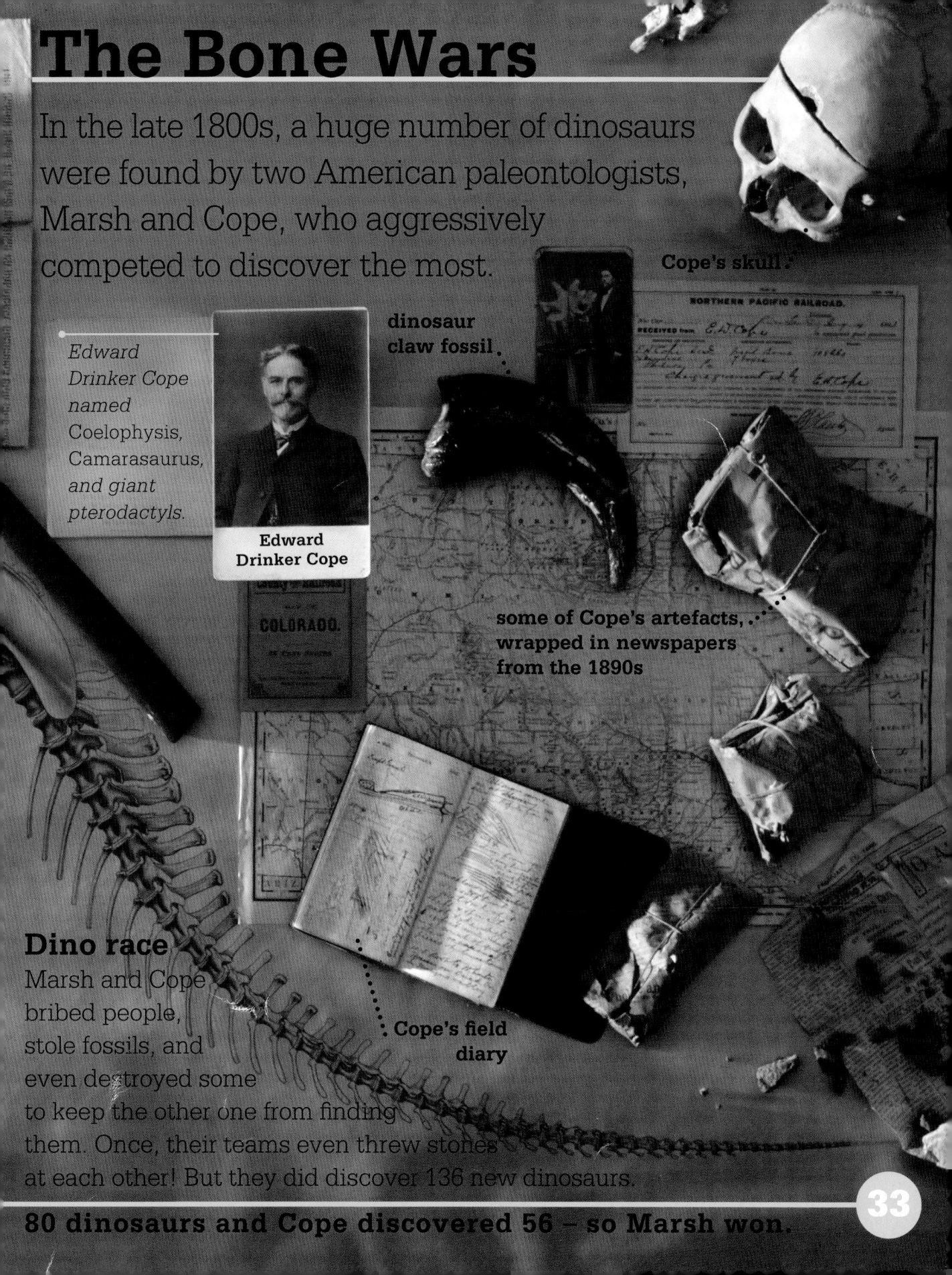


*Edward Drinker Cope named* Coelophysis, Camarasaurus, *and giant pterodactyls.*

## Dino race

Marsh and Cope bribed people, stole fossils, and even destroyed some to keep the other one from finding them. Once, their teams even threw stones at each other! But they did discover 136 new dinosaurs.

**80 dinosaurs and Cope discovered 56 – so Marsh won.**

# Dinosaur eggs

Dinosaurs laid eggs. We know this because egg fossils and nests have been found. Some nests still had fossilized eggs and young in them.

## Giant egg

This huge egg, found in China and thought to be from a therizinosaur, is the biggest dinosaur egg ever found.

## *Maiasaura*

Lots of *Maiasaura* nests have been found in Montana, USA. The nests – holes scooped out of the mud – are near one another, indicating that *Maiasaura* lived in groups.

Maiasaura *young found in nests had weak legs, which means that the mother had to feed and care for her babies.*

**Find out more** about *Protoceratops* on pages 56–57.



**The Montana site where many *Maiasaura***

## *Oviraptor*

This fossil was found in the Gobi Desert, Mongolia. It shows an *Oviraptor* sitting on her nest of eggs. She probably sat on them to keep them warm and safe, just like birds do today.

*Scientists think that dino eggs were leathery and soft – more like reptile eggs than bird eggs.*

## *Protoceratops*

*Protoceratops* laid its eggs in the hot sands of the Gobi Desert. A fossil *Protoceratops* nest with 12 eggs in it has been found.

**nests have been found is called Egg Mountain.**

# Diplodocus

Diplodocus *moved very slowly on all four of its thick legs.*

By the Jurassic period, the giants had appeared. *Diplodocus* was a member of the super-huge sauropod group.

*It is thought that* Diplodocus *laid its eggs while walking along!*

**DIPLODOCUS**
**(DI-plod-oh-kuss)**

**NAME MEANING:**
"Double beam"

**PERIOD:**
Jurassic

**DIET:** Plants

## Teeth

*Diplodocus* had small, peg-shaped teeth at the front of its jaws, to tear off leaves. It had no back teeth, so it would have swallowed without chewing.

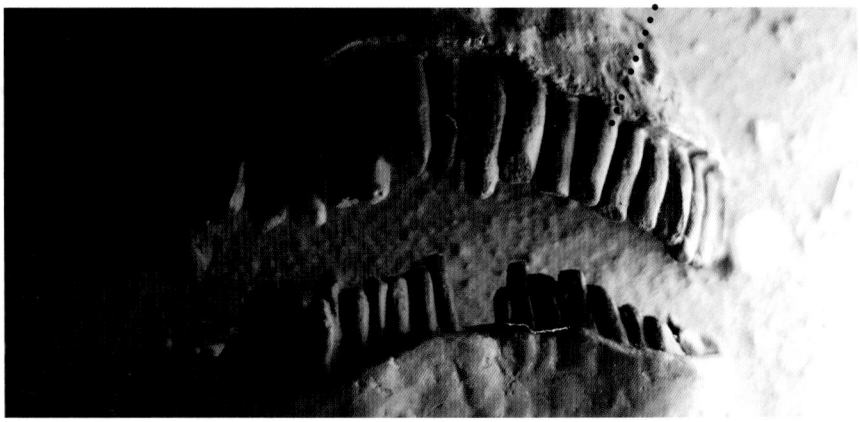




***Diplodocus* would have swallowed small stones**

## Big eater

*Diplodocus* had an appetite as large as its body. It probably ate for up to 20 hours a day to maintain its massive body size.

Diplodocus *was about as long as two school buses!*

Diplodocus *had a long tail that it could have used to whip its enemies.*

**Find out more** about sauropods on the next pages.

## Footprints

Fossil footprints of sauropods walking together tell us that they lived in herds. Imagine seeing a herd of *Diplodocus* dinosaurs walking by!

*Each footprint is as big as a child's bathtub.*

**to help grind up the unchewed plants in its stomach.**

# Super giants

The sauropods were the longest, tallest, and heaviest animals EVER to live on land. They were huge!

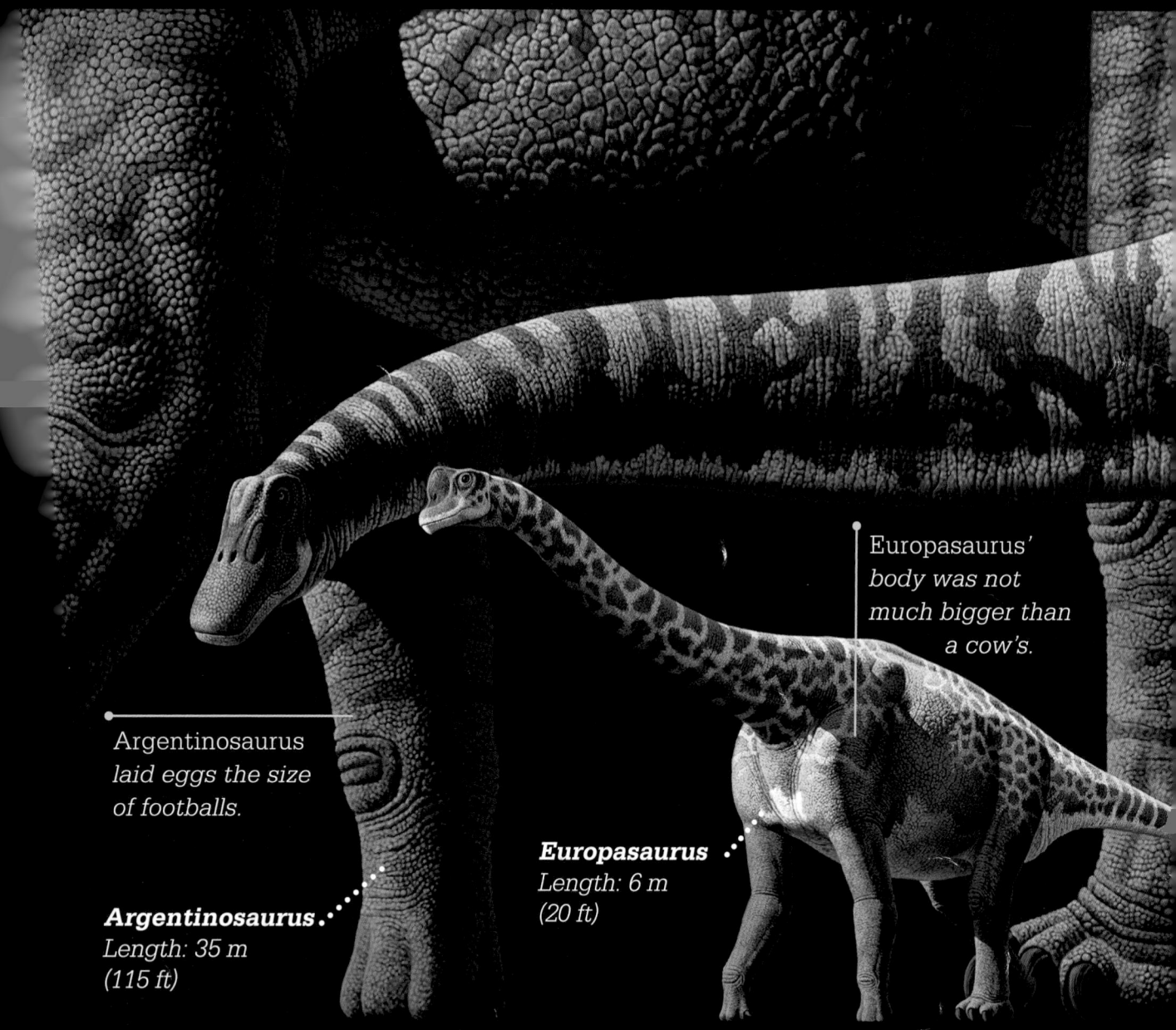


## rgentinosaurus

*gentinosaurus* was probably the ggest sauropod, dinosaur, and land imal of all. It was truly colossal – it weighed as much as 14 elephants!

## *Europasaurus*

Bones from *Europasaurus* were thought to be from a baby sauropod until scientists realized they were actually from an adult mini-sauropod.

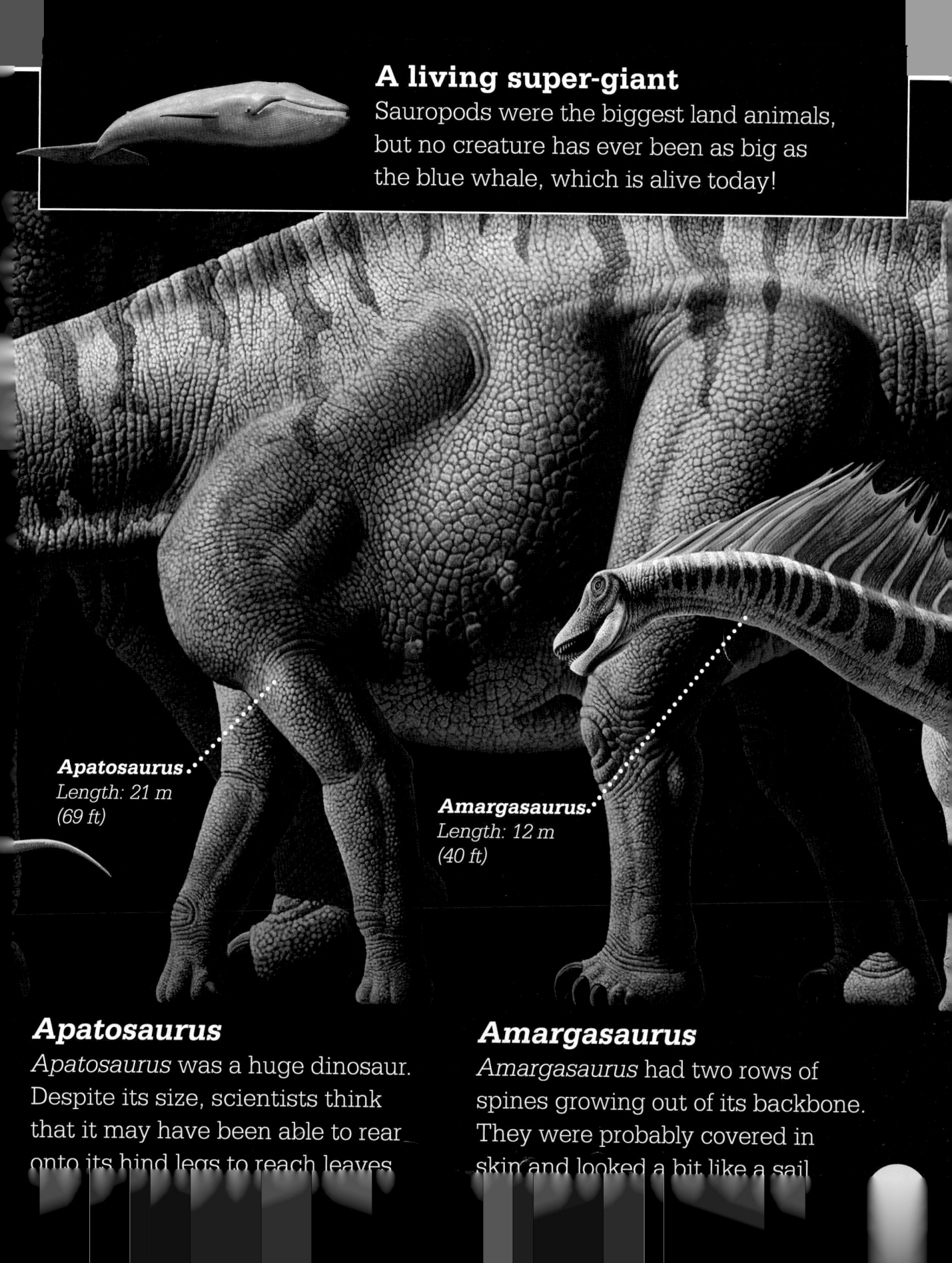


## A living super-giant

Sauropods were the biggest land animals, but no creature has ever been as big as the blue whale, which is alive today!

## *Apatosaurus*

*Apatosaurus* was a huge dinosaur. Despite its size, scientists think that it may have been able to rear onto its hind legs to reach leaves

## *Amargasaurus*

*Amargasaurus* had two rows of spines growing out of its backbone. They were probably covered in skin and looked a bit like a sail

# Compsognathus

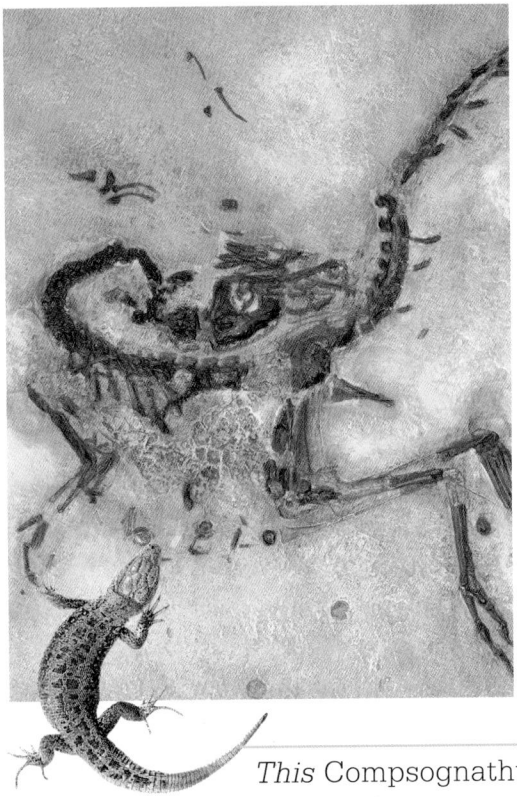

*Compsognathus* is one of the smallest dinosaurs ever found. It was fast, a meat-eater, and about the size of a turkey.

## Lizard lunch

This *Compsognathus* fossil has a lizard in its stomach. The lizard was a fast-moving one, so this dinosaur must have been a quick hunter with good eyesight.

*This* Compsognathus*'s last meal was a* Bavarisaurus, *like this lizard.*

*A fossil showing part of the skin on* Compsognathus*' tail suggests that it was scaly.*

## Small but deadly

*Compsognathus* was a fierce little dinosaur with a small head and a mouth filled with sharp, deadly teeth.

***Compsognathus***

**Find out more** about an even smaller dinosaur on pages 58–59.



**Two complete *Compsognathus* skeletons were found in**

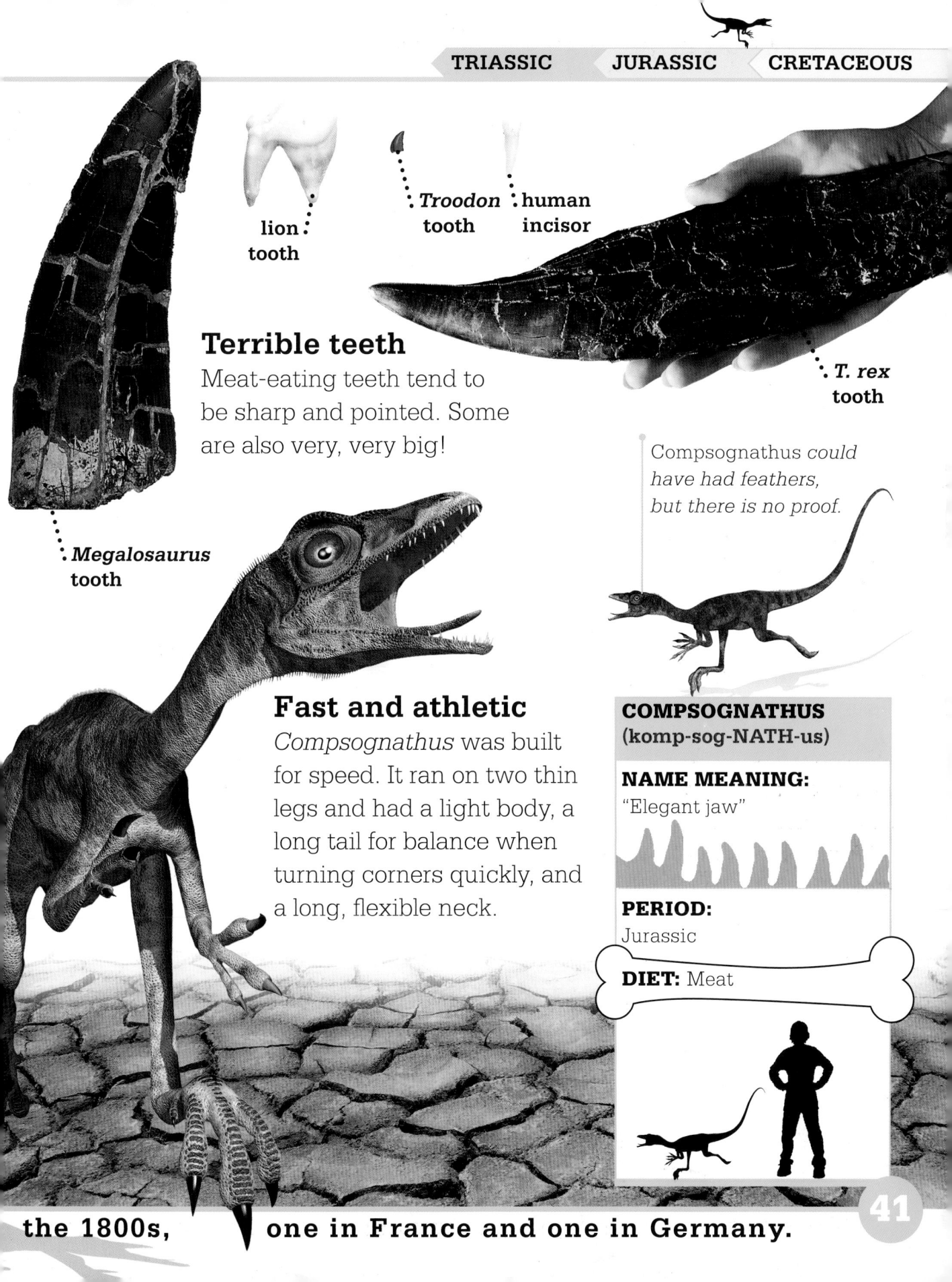


## Terrible teeth

Meat-eating teeth tend to be sharp and pointed. Some are also very, very big!

## Fast and athletic

*Compsognathus* was built for speed. It ran on two thin legs and had a light body, a long tail for balance when turning corners quickly, and a long, flexible neck.

the 1800s, one in France and one in Germany.

# *Stegosaurus* vs

*Stegosaurus* was a giant plant-eating dinosaur with huge plates across its back. It was pretty big, but it still had to watch out for *Allosaurus*!

## The fight

If *Allosaurus* managed to kill *Stegosaurus*, it had enough to eat for weeks. Let's find out how they might have fought.

**STEGOSAURUS**
**(STEG-oh-SORE-us)**

**NAME MEANING:**
"Roof lizard"

**DIET:** Plants

**ALLOSAURUS**
**(AL-oh-SORE-us)**

**NAME MEANING:**
"Other lizard"

**DIET:** Meat

**PERIOD:**
Jurassic

*Tough skin protected* Stegosaurus *from sharp teeth.*

***Stegosaurus***

*Huge, thick legs to support a heavy body made* Stegosaurus *slow.*



**Result: Physically they were evenly matched, but**

# Allosaurus

**Find out more** about *Velociraptor* vs *Protoceratops* on pages 56–57.

***Allosaurus* had a bigger brain, so it used its wits to win.**

# Jurassic rock Welcome to a giant fossil

*If you visit the area, you can still see about 1,500 bones embedded in the rock.*



**Paleontologists carefully remove the rock to find the**

quarry – Dinosaur National Monument, in Utah, USA.

**Fossils**

This amazing quarry has produced more Jurassic dinosaur fossils – including *Stegosaurus*, *Apatosaurus*, and the giant meat-eater *Allosaurus* – than anywhere else in the world.

**fossils. Can you spot any bones around them?**

# Cretaceous dinosaurs

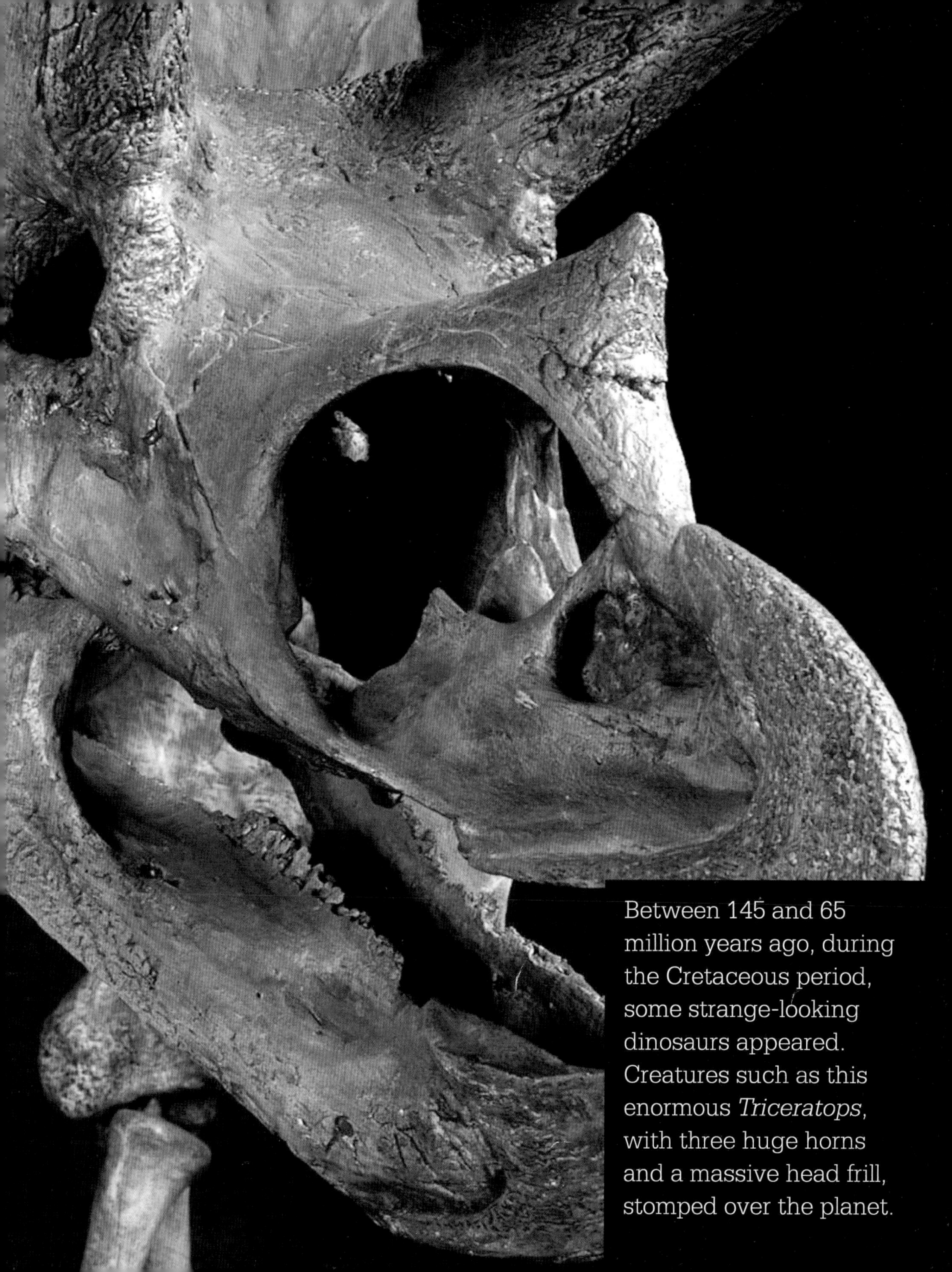

Between 145 and 65 million years ago, during the Cretaceous period, some strange-looking dinosaurs appeared. Creatures such as this enormous *Triceratops*, with three huge horns and a massive head frill, stomped over the planet.

# Cretaceous collection

During the Cretaceous period, there was a huge variety of dinosaurs. There were big ones and small ones – some with crests, horns, or spines.

Struthiosaurus
Torosaurus
Rhabdodon
Baryonyx
Isisaurus
Gallimimus
Polacanthus
Oviraptor
Edmontonia
Psittacosaurus
Dromaeosaurus
Brachylophosaurus
Ouranosaurus
Mononykus

# Iguanodon



*Iguanodon* was one of the first dinosaurs to be discovered. It was first found in England but has since turned up all over the world.

## Worldwide dinosaur

*Iguanodon* was once a very common animal on Earth. Its bones have been found in North Africa, Central Asia, and North America, as well as in Europe.

## *Iguanodon* herds

Many *Iguanodon* fossils have been found together, which suggests that they lived in big herds.



***Iguanodon* could run quite fast on two or four legs.**

# Spinosaurus

*Spinosaurus* would have been a frightening sight, with its dragon-like sail and super-sharp teeth.

## Fish-eater

Scientists thought that dinosaurs ate only meat or plants, until they discovered *Spinosaurus* – it was a meat-eater that caught and ate fish, too.

**SPINOSAURUS**
**(SPINE-oh-SORE-us)**

**NAME MEANING:**
"Spine lizard"

**PERIOD:**
Cretaceous

**DIET:** Meat and fish

## Fishing dinosaur

*Spinosaurus* had sharp claws, and long jaws with knife-edged teeth – both ideal for catching slippery fish.

**Spinosaurus was ENORMOUS! It was as big as *T. rex***

# Edmontosaurus

*Edmontosaurus* was a massive hadrosaur, or duck-billed dinosaur. It was a plant-eater that lived in large herds in swampy areas.

**Quick senses**

*Edmontosaurus* was a slow-moving dinosaur, but its skull shows that it may have had good eyesight, hearing, and sense of smell – to keep it alert to large reptiles lurking in the water!



Using the latest technology, scientists have discovered

## Hadrosaurs

Hadrosaurs are well known for crests on their skulls. Some may have used their hollow crests for display, or as trumpets that could make loud calls.

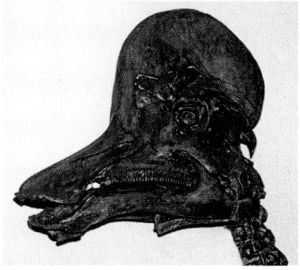

*Corythosaurus* had a large plate-like crest.

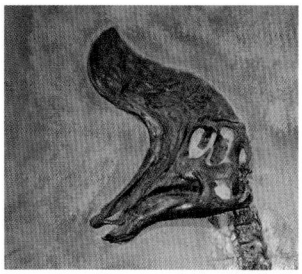

*Lambeosaurus* had a forward-pointing crest.

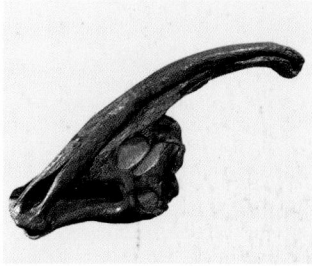

*Parasaurolophus* had a long, hollow crest.

Edmontosaurus *may have had loose skin around its nose, which it might have blown out like a balloon as a display or to make calls.*

Edmontosaurus *had a bumpy ridge down its back.*

**EDMONTOSAURUS**
**(ed-MON-toh-SORE-us)**

**NAME MEANING:** "Lizard of Edmonton (Canada)"

**PERIOD:** Cretaceous

**DIET:** Plants

**the bones of up to 10,000 *Edmontosaurus* in one area!**

# Amazing skulls

Skull fossils of all shapes and sizes tell us what a dinosaur ate, how well it could see, and even how it defended itself.

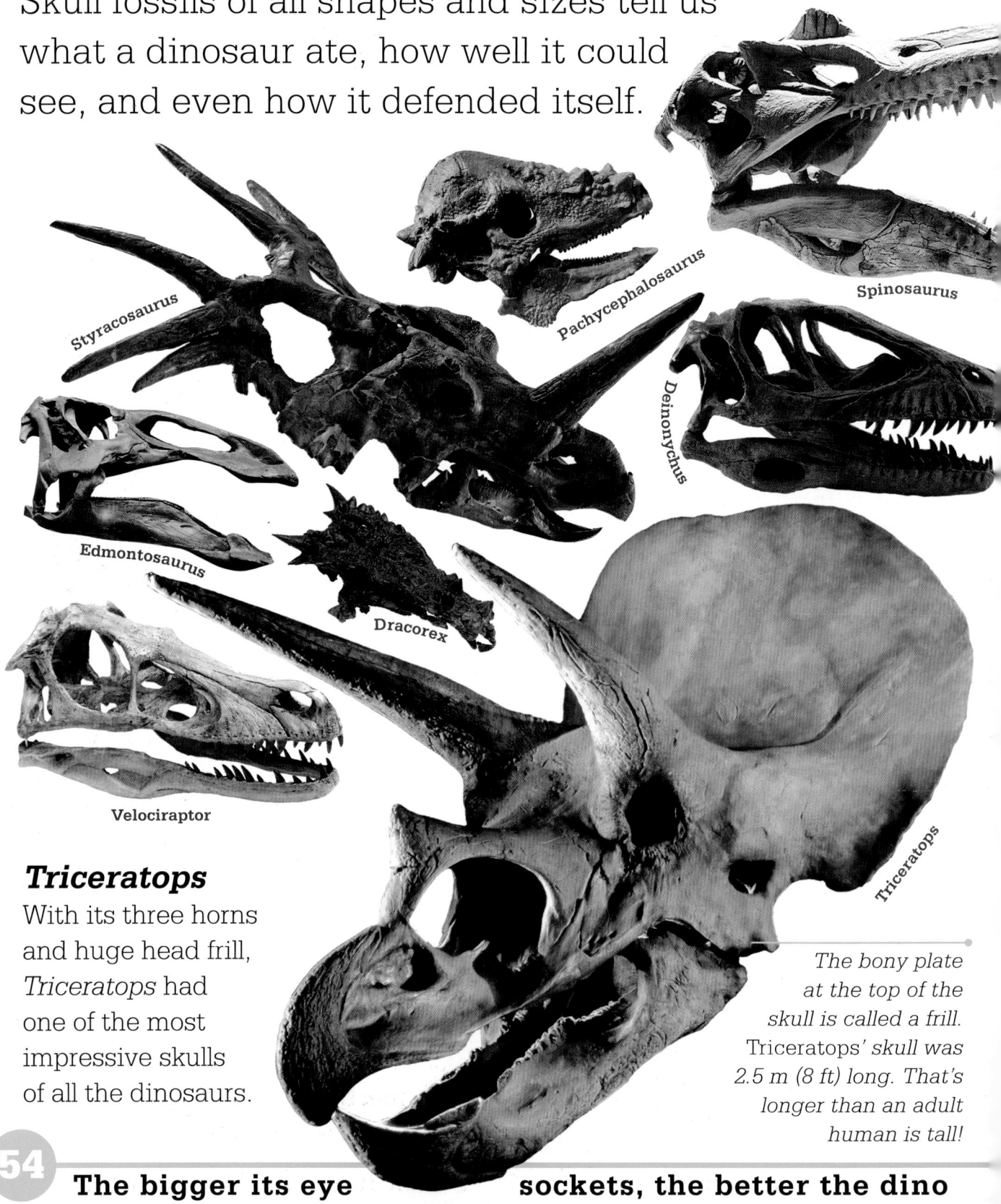


### *Triceratops*

With its three horns and huge head frill, *Triceratops* had one of the most impressive skulls of all the dinosaurs.

*The bony plate at the top of the skull is called a frill.* Triceratops' *skull was 2.5 m (8 ft) long. That's longer than an adult human is tall!*



**The bigger its eye sockets, the better the dino**

### *T. rex*

*T. rex*'s skull was about 1.5 m (5 ft) long. Its eye sockets were 10 cm (4 ins) across, which means that its eyeballs were the size of tennis balls!

**could see. Which do you think had good eyesight?**

# *Velociraptor* vs *Protoceratops*

*Velociraptor* was a small but ferocious predator that probably hunted in packs. Survival was tricky for dinosaurs like *Protoceratops* when *Velociraptor* was hungry.

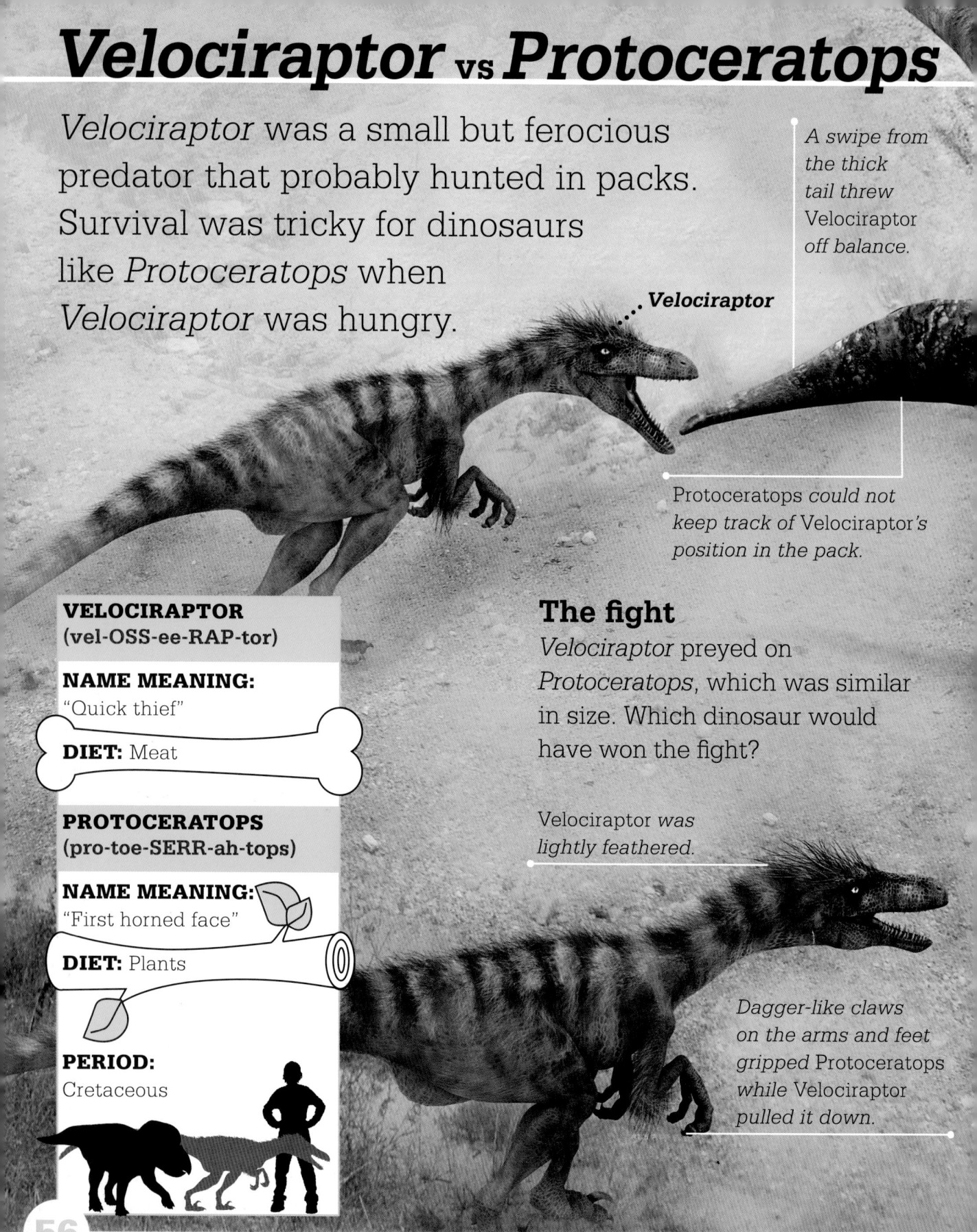


**VELOCIRAPTOR**
**(vel-OSS-ee-RAP-tor)**

**NAME MEANING:**
"Quick thief"

**DIET:** Meat

**PROTOCERATOPS**
**(pro-toe-SERR-ah-tops)**

**NAME MEANING:**
"First horned face"

**DIET:** Plants

**PERIOD:**
Cretaceous

## The fight

*Velociraptor* preyed on *Protoceratops*, which was similar in size. Which dinosaur would have won the fight?

**Result: *Protoceratops* could have wounded *Velociraptor*,**

## Dino fight

In 1971, a double fossil was found in the Gobi Desert, Mongolia – a *Velociraptor* and a *Protoceratops* locked in battle.



**but a lone *Protoceratops* stood no chance against a pack.**

# Gliding dinosaurs

*Microraptor*, discovered in China in 2000, is the smallest dinosaur ever found. It had feathers on its arms and legs and is thought to have glided through forests with all of its limbs stretched out.

*The diamond-shaped tail would have helped keep the dinosaur stable while gliding.*

*Nobody knows what colour the feathers were. They could have been brightly coloured.*

**Dino-birds**

Many paleontologists think that *Microraptor* was an ancestor of the modern birds that we know today.

Microraptor *had claws on its forewings, which it probably used to climb up trees.*

# Ankylosaurs

*Ankylosaurus* and *Gastonia* were both ankylosaurs. Despite being slow-moving plant-eaters, ankylosaurs were super-tough and built for self-defence.

*A swipe of the tail could cause a bad injury.*

***Ankylosaurus***

***Gastonia***

*This dinosaur might not have won any running races, but it was agile enough to swing its clubbed tail.*

Gastonia *had bony plates to protect its eyes.*

**ANKYLOSAURUS**
**(an-KIE-loh-SORE-us)**

**NAME MEANING:**
"Stiff lizard"

**PERIOD:**
Cretaceous

**DIET:** Plants

## Body armour

The best defence an ankylosaur had was its own body. It was a heavy, stocky dinosaur protected by thick bands of bone, which were studded with bony plates or spines.



**The only way to injure these super-tough dinosaurs**

## How to avoid being eaten

Some ankylosaurs may have lived in groups. Other plant-eating dinosaurs, such as *Protoceratops*, also lived in large herds. They defended one another when under attack.

## Defensive tails

The tail was a key weapon in a dinosaur fight. A quick lash of the tail might take even the fiercest hunter by surprise or cause an injury.

Ankylosaurus *had a bony, club-like tail that gave fierce blows.*

Kentrosaurus *and* Stegosaurus *had spiky tails that could pierce skin.*

Supersaurus *may have used its tail to swipe at enemies.*

**was to flip them over and attack their bellies.**

# Mighty *T. rex*

Imagine coming face-to-face with a gigantic head and a mouth full of 58 massive teeth. Say a BIG hello to *Tyrannosaurus rex*!

## King-size dinosaur

*T. rex* was a HUGE dinosaur with a giant head, powerful back legs, and short arms that could barely reach its mouth.

T. rex *was as heavy as 200 eight-year-old children!*

**TYRANNOSAURUS REX**
**(tie-RAN-oh-SORE-us rex)**

**NAME MEANING:**
"Tyrant lizard king"

**PERIOD:**
Cretaceous

**DIET:** Meat

## Terrifying teeth

*T. rex* had teeth with edges as sharp as knives, to cut through flesh, and as thick as bananas, to chomp through bone.

*Its bite was eight times more powerful than a lion's.*

T. rex *could open its mouth incredibly wide and swallow small dinosaurs whole.*

## *T. rex* and friends

It was once thought that *T. rex* lived alone, but evidence found in the Gobi Desert, Mongolia, suggests that *T. rex* may have lived in packs.

# A GIANT DISCOVERY.

## Lucky breakdown

**All because of a flat tyre!**

In the summer of 1990, Sue Hendrickson was looking for fossils in South Dakota when the team of paleontologists she was with got a flat tyre. While it was being changed, Sue wandered off to check out a rock she had spotted earlier. It turned out to hold the biggest *Tyrannosaurus rex* fossil ever discovered. The dinosaur was named Sue.

**Sue lived 67 million**

## The LARGEST and MOST COMPLETE

Turn over the page to discover how the team dug up Sue and rebuilt the complete skeleton.

**Sue Hendrikson and the team with the *T. rex* skull.**

## A great display

The full skeleton displayed in a museum is actually an exact copy of Sue's bones. Her real bones are too precious to display. They are kept safe so that they don't get broken.

years ago

Sue's skull is huge, and so are her teeth. Luckily, she isn't around now to gobble us up!

# *TYRANNOSAURUS REX* ever discovered

## How old is Sue?

Plants were buried and fossilized with Sue, so plant experts looked at them to form an idea about when Sue lived. Geologists (rock experts) also looked at the rocks from which the fossils of the *T. rex* were taken. Together, the scientists worked out that Sue lived about 67 million years ago.

The team used scanners to photograph the bones, then created a digital image of Sue on a computer.

## Bone detectives

By looking at Sue's bones, the team found the following facts:

- Sue received several injuries from fights with other dinosaurs – she even had broken bones that had later healed.
- Her bones showed signs of arthritis, a bone disease that humans can develop as they age.

# Digging up Sue

## Where was Sue?

Sue was discovered in South Dakota, USA, where many fossils have been found. The team also found *Edmontosaurus* fossils there.

## Digging out Sue

The team exposed Sue's bones with tiny tools and brushes that removed the rock around them. It took 6 people 17 days to dig out Sue's bones.

## Cleaning Sue

Fossil specialists carefully cleaned the bones, using tiny instruments. In this picture, Sue's jaw is being cleaned by one of the specialists.

## Mending Sue's bones

The paleontologists studied each bone, and had to mend some of them. Sue's skull had been squashed by rock. It took 3,500 hours to restore it!



**Scientists believe that Sue was 28 years old when she**

## Protecting Sue

A big trench was dug around the bones. Then it was filled with liquid plaster, which turned rock-hard and protected the bones inside.

## Back to the lab

The paleontologists took the bones back to their lab in big trucks. They had to be very careful not to damage the fossils on the way.

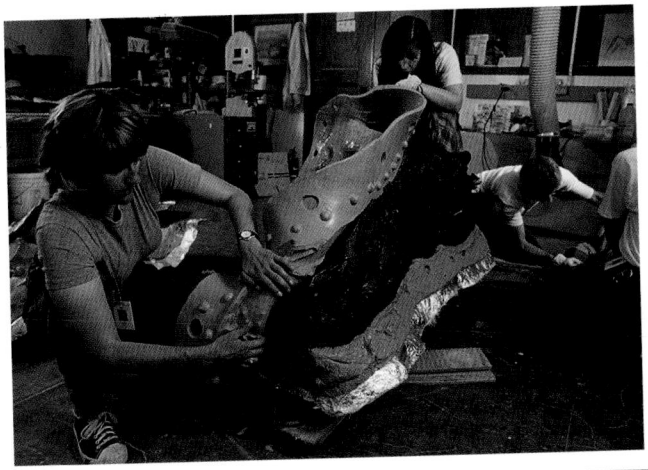

## Filling in gaps

A few of Sue's bones were missing, so paleontologists worked out what they would have looked like and made them out of plastic.

## The complete Sue

Piece by piece, the bones were fitted together into the most complete skeleton of a *T. rex* ever found. A copy is now on display in Chicago, USA.



**died. That was probably very old for a dinosaur.**

# Triceratops

Built like a giant rhinoceros with a huge head, *Triceratops* would have been an awesome sight in Cretaceous times.

## Three horns

*Triceratops* had three big horns, as well as an impressive neck frill. Males probably fought one another for mates, crashing heads and locking horns.

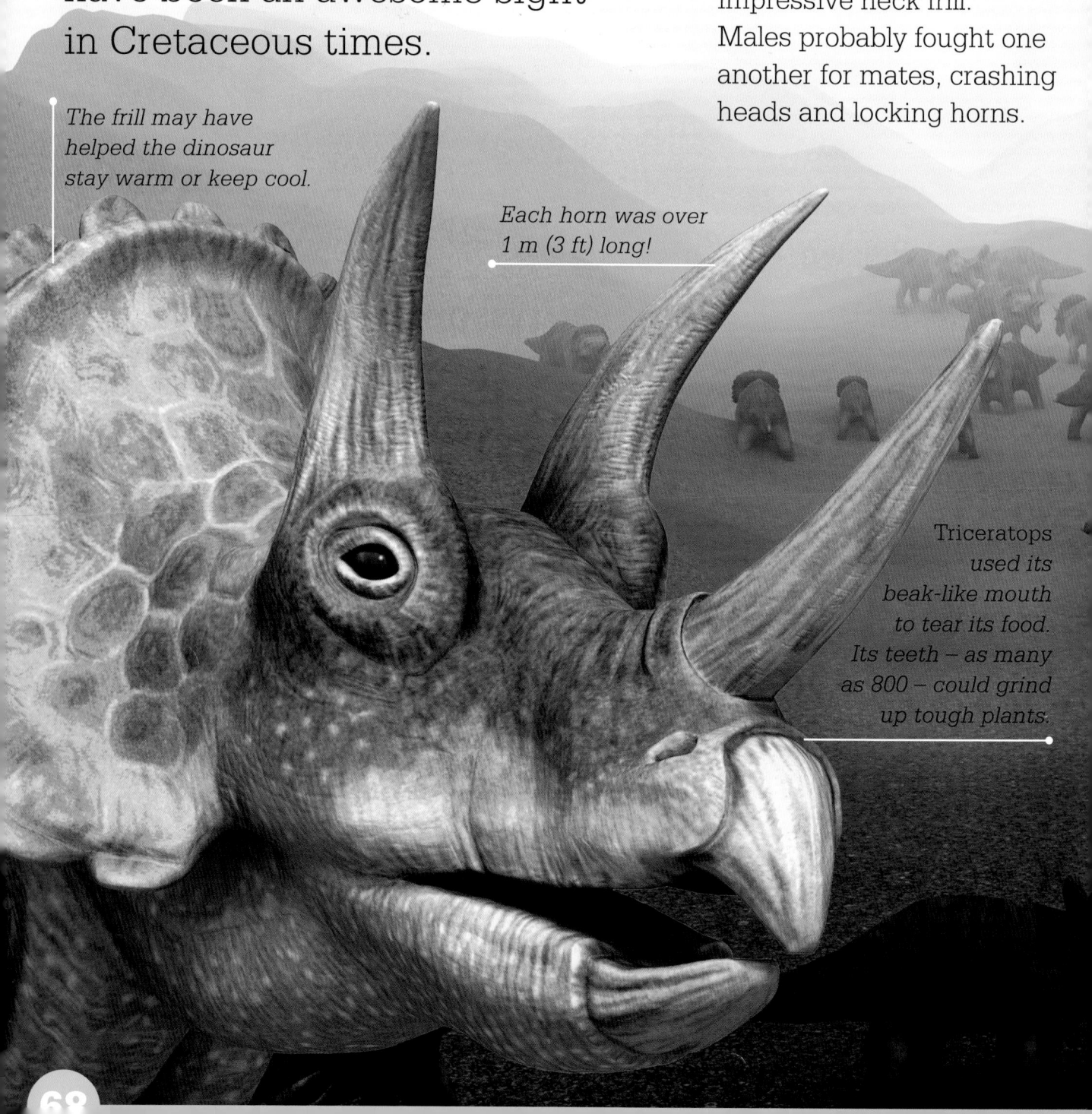

## Amazing heads

*Triceratops* was part of a family called Ceratopsidae, or horn-faced dinosaurs. All of the ceratopsids had impressive heads.

## Defence

*Triceratops* lived in herds for safety and also used its horns for defence. It was strong enough to fight off big hunters, perhaps even *T. rex*.

**TRICERATOPS**
**(tri-SERR-ah-tops)**

**NAME MEANING:**
"Three-horned face"

**PERIOD:**
Cretaceous

**DIET:** Plants

# End of the dinosaurs

Fossils tell us that 65 million years ago, for some reason, many dinosaurs suddenly became extinct, or died out. Nobody knows for sure why it happened.

## Meteorite A disaster from space?

There is some evidence that a giant meteorite (a rock from outer space) crashed into Earth 65 million years ago and hit the Yucatán Peninsula in Mexico.

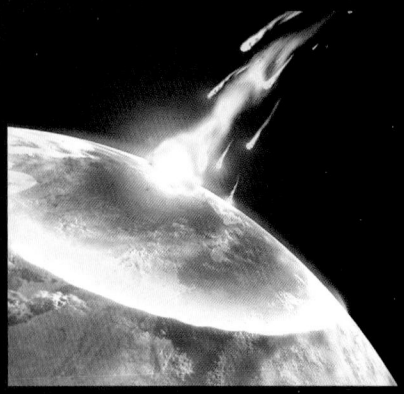

The meteorite would have travelled at 55 km per second (34 miles per second). The impact would have been huge!

The impact would have caused earthquakes, tidal waves, and volcanic eruptions around the world.

A dust cloud from the volcanoes may have killed plants and stopped sunlight from reaching Earth.

ammonites

### Other extinctions

Many flying reptiles, sea reptiles, and other sea creatures (like these ammonites) also died out around the same time, 65 million years ago.



**Many animals survived the meteorite and became the**

*A meteorite impact might have caused the weather to change over time in a way that didn't suit the large dinosaurs.*

**Good-bye, dinosaurs**

No land creature living since has been as big, powerful, and impressive as the mighty dinosaur.

*Terror birds lived in North and South America between 60 and 2 million years ago.*

## Terror bird

These fierce birds, now extinct, were probably related to dinosaurs and to birds alive today.

*The terror bird stood 2.5 m (8 ft) tall.*



**A bird's hollow bones don't fossilize well, so it's hard**

# Dinosaurs today

What if some dinosaurs didn't die out? Many people think that birds are related to dinosaurs.

### *Archaeopteryx*

*Archaeopteryx*, a dinosaur alive in the Jurassic period, was the earliest known bird. It had feathers, but also teeth and a bony tail.

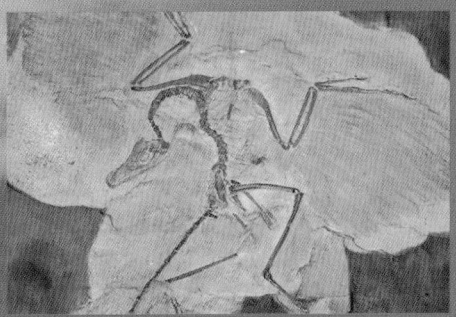

### Hoatzin

A hoatzin chick has claws on its wings that it uses to crawl up trees – maybe like *Archaeopteryx* did.

### Chicken

Scientists recently compared tests of bones from a chicken and a *T. rex* and found that they are quite similar!

### Cassowary

The cassowary of New Guinea and Australia has a horny crest like *Lambeosaurus* (see pages 18–19 and 53).



**to work out how birds have changed over time.**

# History of discovery

It has been only 200 years since scientists learned that dinosaurs existed. New evidence has turned up all over the world.

## 0 CE

*Large bones found in China were thought to belong to fire-breathing dragons. In fact, they were probably dinosaur bones.*

## 1824

*British scientist William Buckland announced that Plot's huge bone belonged to* Megalosaurus, *a species of giant creatures, first called "dinosaurs" in 1841.*

## 1825

*In England, Gideon Mantell discovered the bones of, and named,* Iguanodon.

## 1676

*A huge bone, probably belonging to a dinosaur, was found by Robert Plot in England. He thought it was from a giant human.*

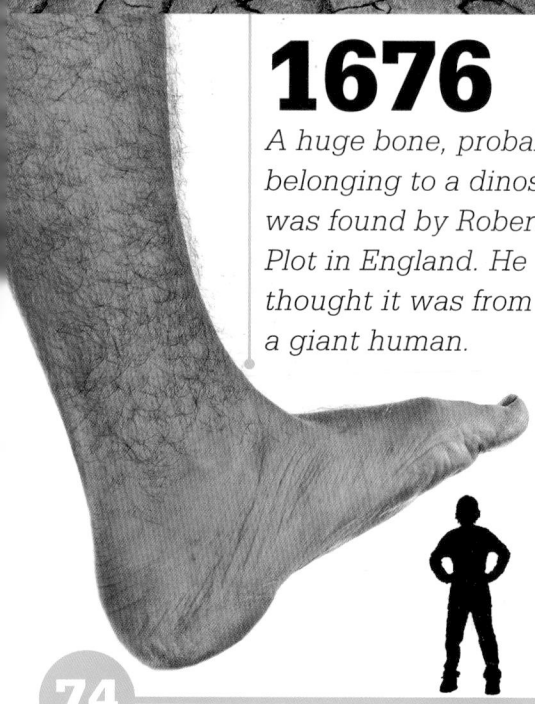

## 1823

*Mary Anning discovered remains of* Plesiosaurus, *a giant sea reptile, near her home in England. This proved that massive animals that are no longer alive today once existed.*

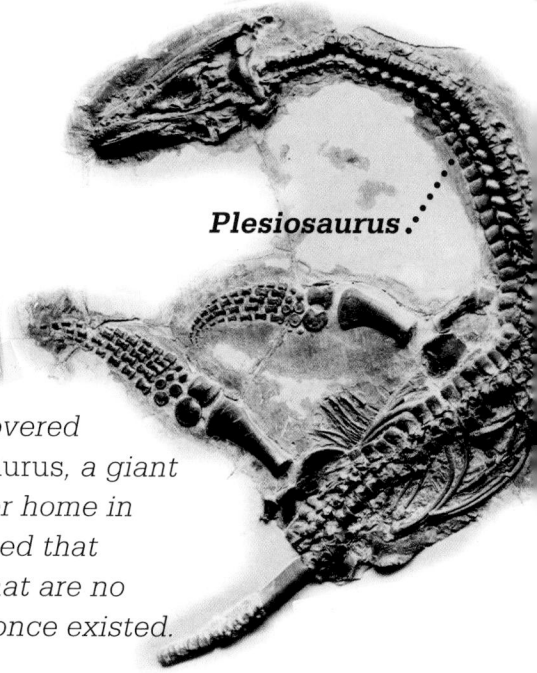




**Recent technology and new fossils are giving us fresh**

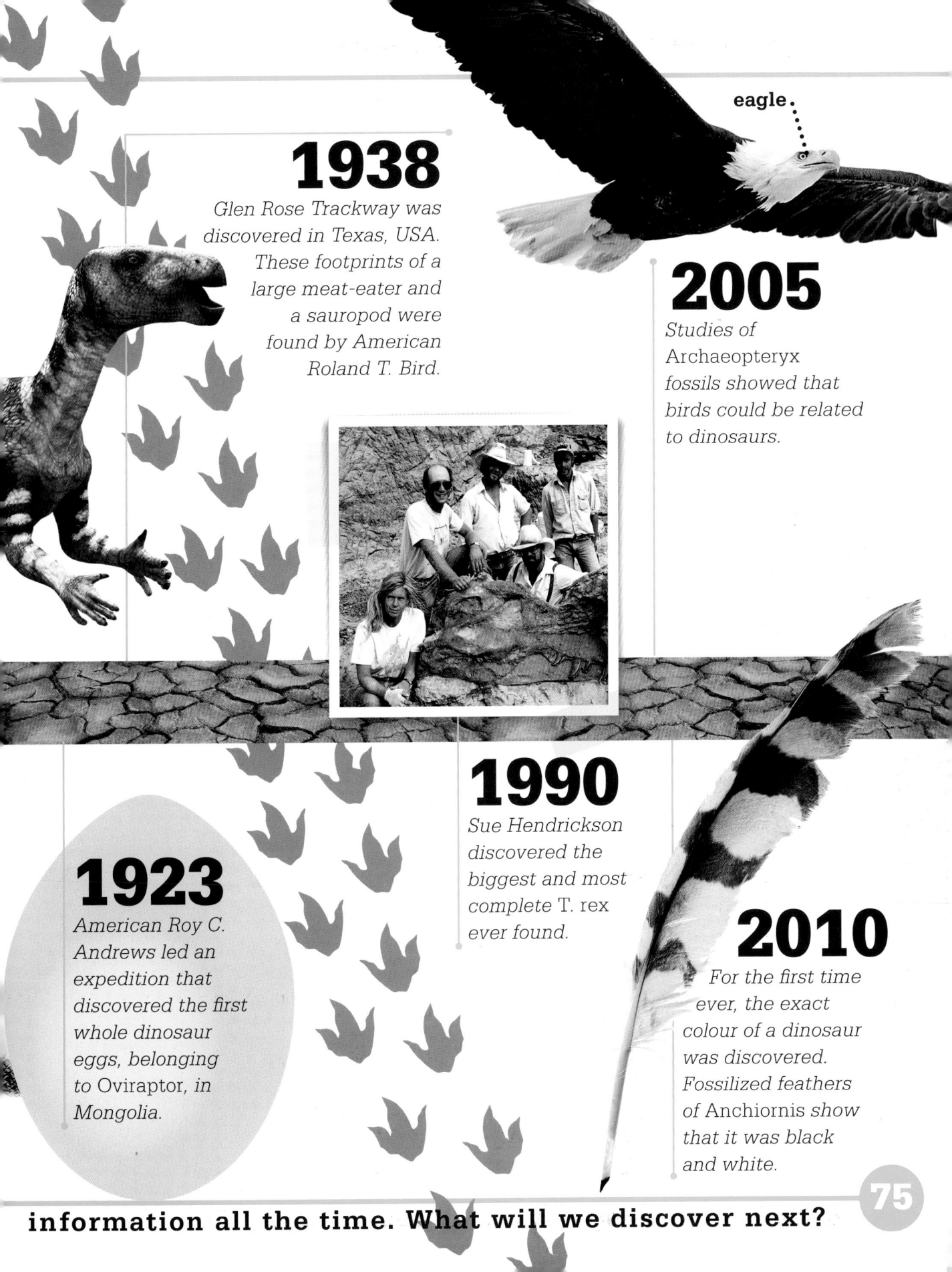


## 1938

*Glen Rose Trackway was discovered in Texas, USA. These footprints of a large meat-eater and a sauropod were found by American Roland T. Bird.*

## 2005

*Studies of* Archaeopteryx *fossils showed that birds could be related to dinosaurs.*

## 1990

*Sue Hendrickson discovered the biggest and most complete* T. rex *ever found.*

## 1923

*American Roy C. Andrews led an expedition that discovered the first whole dinosaur eggs, belonging to* Oviraptor, *in Mongolia.*

## 2010

*For the first time ever, the exact colour of a dinosaur was discovered. Fossilized feathers of* Anchiornis *show that it was black and white.*

**information all the time. What will we discover next?**

# Pronunciation guide

***Allosaurus***
AL-oh-SORE-us

***Amargasaurus***
A-MARG-ah-SORE-us

***Anchiornis***
an-KEY-or-nis

***Ankylosaurus***
ang-KIE-loh-SORE-us

***Apatosaurus***
ah-PAT-oh-SORE-us

***Archaeopteryx***
ark-ee-OPT-er-ix

***Argentinosaurus***
AR-gent-een-oh-SORE-us

***Bavarisaurus***
ba-VAIR-ih-SORE-us

***Camarasaurus***
KAM-ar-ah-SORE-us

**Ceratopsidae**
serr-ah-TOP-si-day

***Ceratosaurus***
seh-RAT-oh-SORE-us

***Coelophysis***
seel-OH-fie-sis

***Compsognathus***
komp-sog-NATH-us

***Corythosaurus***
koh-RITH-oh-SORE-us

**cycnodont**
SIE-no-dont

***Deinonychus***
die-NON-i-kuss

***Dimetrodon***
DIE-me-troh-don

***Diplodocus***
DI-plod-oh-kuss

***Dromaeosaurus***
DROM-ee-oh-SORE-us

***Edmontosaurus***
ed-MON-toh-SORE-us

***Europasaurus***
you-ROH-pah-SORE-us

***Gallimimus***
gal-lee-meem-us

***Gastonia***
gas-TOH-nee-ah

***Giganotosaurus***
gi-gan-OH-toe-SORE-us

**hadrosaur**
HAD-row-sore

***Herrerasaurus***
herr-ray-rah-SORE-us

***ichthyosaur***
ICK-thee-oh-sore

***Iguanodon***
ig-WHA-noh-don

***Kentrosaurus***
ken-TROH-SORE-us

***Lambeosaurus***
lam-BEE-oh-SORE-us

***Liopleurodon***
LIE-oh-PLER-oh-don

***Maiasaura***
my-ah-SORE-ah

***Megalosaurus***
MEG-ah-low-SORE-us

***Micropachycephalosaurus***
mike-row-pak-ee-SEF-ah-loh-SORE-us

***Microraptor***
mike-row-RAP-tor

***Oviraptor***
OH-vee-RAP-tor

***Pachycephalosaurus***
pack-ee-SEF-al-oh-SORE-us

***Parasaurolophus***
pa-ra-SAW-ROL-off-us

***Plesiosaurus***
PLEEZ-ee-oh-SORE-us

***Protoceratops***
pro-toe-SERR-ah-tops

**pterodactyl**
terr-oh-DAC-til

**pterosaur**
terr-oh-sore

**sauropod**
SORE-oh-pod

***Spinosaurus***
SPINE-oh-SORE-us

***Stegosaurus***
STEG-oh-SORE-us

***Supersaurus***
SUE-per-SORE-us

***Therizinosaurus***
THER-ih-ZINE-oh-SORE-us

***Torosaurus***
tor-oh-SORE-us

***Triceratops***
tri-SERR-ah-tops

***Troodon***
TROH-oh-don

***Tyrannosaurus rex***
tie-RAN-oh-SORE-us rex

***Velociraptor***
vell-OSS-ee-RAP-tor

# Glossary

**coprolite**
Animal poo that has been turned into a fossil.

**dinosaur**
An often very large reptile with four limbs and scaly or feathered skin. Dinosaurs laid eggs and lived on land. Dinosaurs died out 65 million years ago, but their descendants, birds, are alive today.

**era**
A very long span of time in Earth's history.

**extinct**
No longer in existence, having died out.

**fossil**
The ancient remains of an animal or plant that lived many years ago. A fossil may be animal remains, footprints, or even a plant, preserved within rock.

**frill**
A large, fan-like flap of skin and bone that some dinosaurs had on their heads or necks.

**herd**
A group of animals that live or travel together.

**ichthyosaur**
A large, swimming reptile that existed at the same time as the dinosaurs.

**meteorite**
A piece of rock or metal from space that crashes on Earth.

**paleontologist**
A scientist who studies prehistoric life.

**predator**
An animal that hunts and eats other animals.

**prey**
An animal that is eaten by other animals.

**pterosaur**
A flying reptile with bat-like wings made of stretched skin. They lived at the same time as the dinosaurs.

**reptile**
A cold-blooded animal with scaly skin that lays eggs. Snakes and crocodiles are reptiles, as were dinosaurs.

**sauropod**
A gentle, plant-eating dinosaur, often very large, with a long neck and a long, whip-like tail.

**skeleton**
The complete set of bones in an animal's body.

*This* Protoceratops *baby is emerging from its egg.*

# Index


**A**

*Allosaurus* 12–13, 24–25, 26–27, 32, 42–43, 45
*Amargasaurus* 39, 48
*Anchiornis* 75
Andrews, Roy C. 75
ankylosaur 60–61
*Ankylosaurus* 11, 17, 60
Anning, Mary 74
*Apatosaurus* 27, 38–39, 45
*Archaeopteryx* 26, 73, 75
Argentina 14, 30
*Argentinosaurus* 10–11, 38–39

**B**

baby dinosaur 9, 34–35, 77
bird 20, 35, 58, 72–73, 75
Bird, Roland T. 75
Buckland, William 74

**C**

Canada 16, 17, 18, 53
*Camarasaurus* 8–9, 33
Cenozoic era 13
Ceratopsidae 69
*Ceratosaurus* 32–33
China 16, 34, 58, 74
claws 9, 11, 33, 43, 51, 56–57, 59, 73
*Coelophysis* 12, 14, 31, 33
colour 9, 58, 75
*Compsognathus* 15, 27, 40–41
Cope, Edward Drinker 32–33
*Corythosaurus* 48, 53
Cretaceous period 12–13, 19, 46–49, 78

**D**

defence 11, 15, 17, 37, 42–43, 50, 60–61, 69
*Deinonychus* 11, 54
Dinosaur National Monument 44–45
*Diplodocus* 14–15, 32, 36–37
*Dromaeosaurus* 49, 78

**E**

*Edmontosaurus* 16, 52–53, 54, 66
egg 10, 21, 34–35, 36, 38, 75, 77
England 50, 74
*Europasaurus* 38
extinction 12–13, 28, 70–71, 72, 77
eyes 19, 31, 52, 54–55, 60

**F**

feathers 8, 9, 16, 20, 41, 56, 58, 59, 73, 75
feeding 21, 36–37, 39, 54, 63, 68
fighting 22, 25, 33, 42–43, 56–57, 60–61, 65, 68
fish 12, 21, 28–29, 51
flying 9, 28–29, 73
footprint 20, 37, 75
fossil 6–7, 8–9, 10, 11, 14–17, 18–19, 20–21, 22–23, 24–25, 30, 31, 32–33, 34–35, 37, 38, 40–41, 42, 44–45, 46–47, 50, 53, 57, 60–61, 64–67, 74–75, 77
frill 17, 47, 54, 68, 77


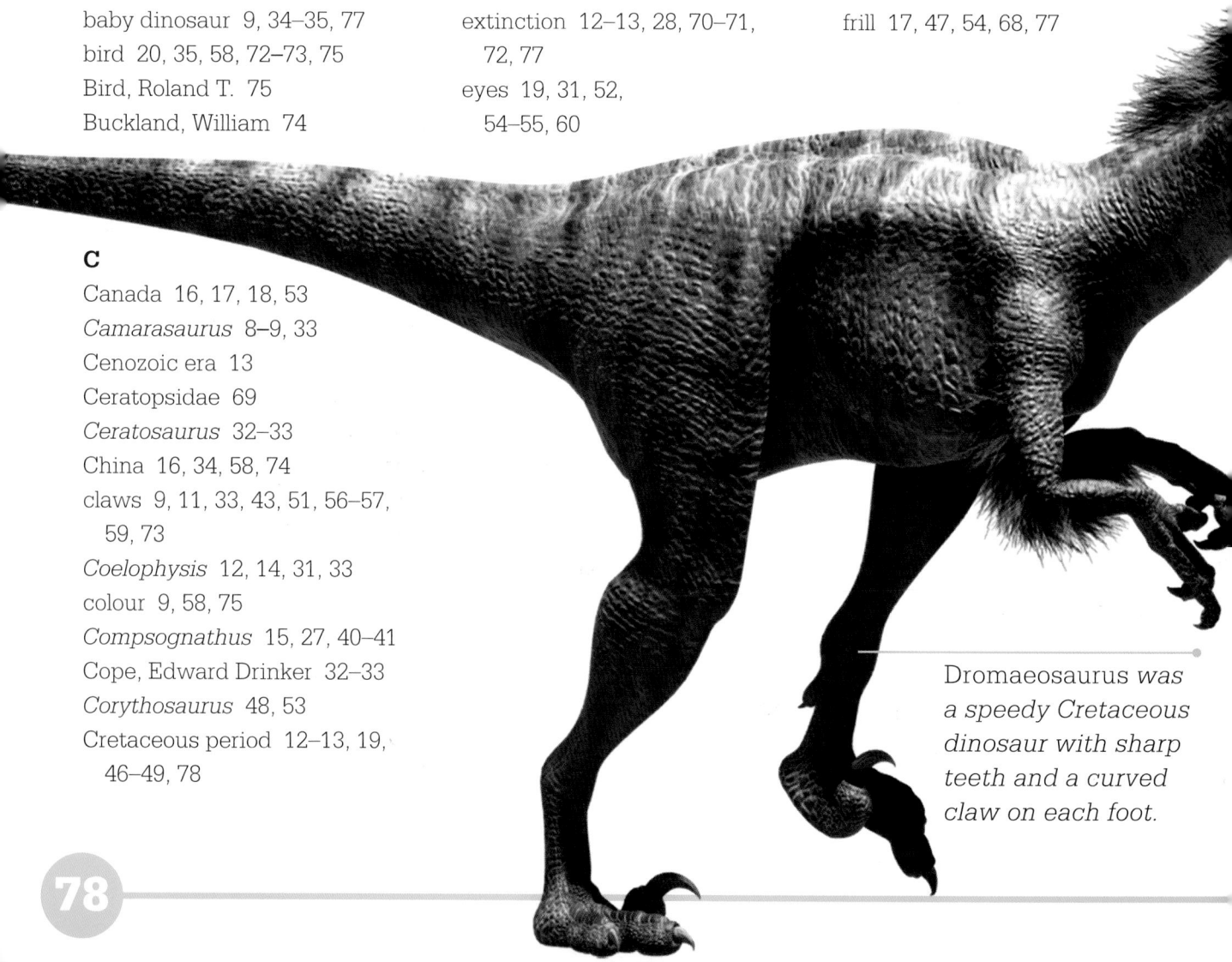

Dromaeosaurus *was a speedy Cretaceous dinosaur with sharp teeth and a curved claw on each foot.*

**G**
*Gallimimus* 10, 49
*Gastonia* 60–61
*Giganotosaurus* 10, 48

**H**
hadrosaur 11, 18, 52–53, 55
Hendrickson, Sue 64, 66, 75
herd 16, 37, 50, 52, 61, 69, 77
Herrera, Victorino 30
*Herrerasaurus* 14, 26, 30
hunting 10, 16, 21, 30, 40, 56–57, 63

**I**
ichthyosaur 29
*Iguanodon* 15, 23, 50, 74–75
insect 12, 29, 35

**J**
Jurassic period 12–13, 24–27, 36, 44–45, 73

**K**
*Kentrosaurus* 26, 61

**L**
*Lambeosaurus* 18–19, 53, 73
limbs 8, 9, 18, 30, 36, 43, 50, 56, 58, 62
*Liopleurodon* 28–29

**M**
*Maiasaura* 10, 34–35
mammal 12, 13, 21, 29, 39, 47
Mantell, Gideon 23, 74
Marsh, Othniel Charles 32–33
meat-eater 7, 9, 10, 14–17, 26, 28, 30, 31, 40, 41, 42, 45, 51, 56, 62–63
*Megalosaurus* 41, 74
Mesozoic era 13
meteorite 70–71
Mexico 18, 70
*Microraptor* 11, 58–59
Mongolia 16, 17, 35, 57, 63, 75

**N**
nest 34–35

**O**
*Oviraptor* 35, 49, 75

**PQ**
*Pachycephalosaurus* 22–23, 54
paleontologist 18, 20–21, 22–23, 32–33, 44, 52–53, 58, 64–67, 74–75, 77
Paleozoic era 12
*Parasaurolophus* 53, 55
plant-eater 8, 11, 14–17, 19, 21, 26, 36, 39, 42, 50, 52–53, 56, 60, 68–69
*Plesiosaurus* 74
Plot, Robert 74
Precambrian era 12
*Protoceratops* 35, 55, 56–57, 61, 77
pterosaur 28–29

**R**
reptile 8, 12–13, 27, 28–29, 31, 35, 40, 52, 70, 74, 77
running 10, 18, 20, 30, 41, 43, 50, 60

**S**
sauropod 9, 36–39, 75
skin 8, 9, 11, 20, 39, 42, 57
skull 6–7, 10, 22–23, 30, 52, 53, 54–55, 60, 64–65, 66
*Spinosaurus* 16, 51, 54–55, 60
*Stegosaurus* 15, 24–25, 32, 42–43, 45, 61
"Sue" (T. rex) 64–67, 75
*Supersaurus* 61

**T**
tail 9, 11, 17, 30, 37, 41, 42, 43, 56, 58, 60–61, 73
teeth 7, 9, 11, 17, 19, 30, 36, 40, 41, 42–43, 50, 51, 57, 62, 63, 68, 73
*Therizinosaurus* 11
*Torosaurus* 10, 49
Triassic period 12–13, 24–27, 30–31
*Triceratops* 17, 32, 46–47, 54, 68–69
*Troodon* 41, 48
*Tyrannosaurus rex* 6–7, 8–9, 17, 41, 51, 55, 62–67, 69, 73, 75

**U**
United States 14–17, 18, 31, 32–33, 34, 66, 75

**VWXYZ**
*Velociraptor* 13, 16, 54, 56–57, 78

# Thank you


### Photography

6–7: Dorling Kindersley/Getty Images; 8bl: defpicture/Shutterstock; 9cr: Louie Psihoyos/Getty Images; 10–11 (background): Nataliia Natykach/Shutterstock; 10–11 (all frames): Iakov Filimonov/Shutterstock; 11tr: Francois Gohier/Photo Researchers, Inc.; 12 (dragonfly): Media Bakery; 13 (human): Image Source/Corbis; 18–19: Stephen J Krasemann/age fotostock; 19cl: Mark Garlick/Science Photo Library; 19cr: Francois Gohier/Photo Researchers, Inc.; 20tl: thinkdo/Shutterstock; 20tr: Terence Walsh/Shutterstock; 20bl: Francois Gohier/Photo Researchers, Inc.; 20bc: Vladimir Sazonov/Shutterstock; 20br: Mariya Bibikova/iStockphoto; 21tl: Ted Kinsman/Photo Researchers, Inc.; 21tr: Sinclair Stammers/Photo Researchers, Inc.; 21bl: British Antarctic Survey/Science Photo Library; 21br: Philip Hattingh/iStockphoto; 22–23 (skull): Jim Lane/Alamy; 23tr: Paul D Stewart/Science Photo Library; 23cr: Science Source/Photo Researchers, Inc.; 24–25: All rights reserved, Image Archives, Denver Museum of Nature & Science; 29crt: iStockphoto/Thinkstock; 30br: Boris Mrdja/iStockphoto; 32–33 (all): Louie Psihoyos/Science Faction/Corbis; 34l: Louie Psihoyos/Corbis; 35t: AP Photo/Denis Finnin and Mick Ellison, copyright American Museum of Natural History; 36br: Chris Waits/flickr; 37bl: Francois Gohier/Photo Researchers, Inc.; 37br: Gamma-Keystone via Getty Images; 40tl: NHPA/SuperStock; 40cl: iStockphoto/Thinkstock; 41tr: Louie Psihoyos/Getty Images; 41 (all other teeth): Colin Keates/Getty Images; 44–45: Louie Psihoyos/Getty Images; 46–47: Francois Gohier/Photo Researchers, Inc.; 53tl: Albert Copley/Visuals Unlimited/Corbis; 53tc: Stephen J Krasemann/age fotostock; 53tr: D. Gordon E. Robertson/Wikipedia; 54 (*Styracosaurus*): Ira Block/National Geographic/Getty Images; 54 (*Pachycephalosaurus*): Ballista from the English Wikipedia; 54 (*Spinosaurus*): author Kabacchi, uploaded by FunkMonk/Wikipedia; 54 (*Edmontosaurus*): Wikipedia; 54 (*Dracorex*): Wikipedia; 54 (*Deinonychus*): Thinkstock; 54 (*Velociraptor*): Thinkstock; 54 (*Triceratops*): Science Faction/SuperStock; 55 (*Parasaurolophus*): D. Gordon E. Robertson/Wikipedia; 55 (*Ingenia*): Wikipedia; 55 (*Saurolophus*): Natalia Pavlova/Dreamstime; 55 (*Falcarius*): Paul Davies/Dreamstime; 55 (*Tarbosaurus*): Rozenn Leard/Dreamstime; 55 (*Protoceratops*): Francois Gohier/Photo Researchers, Inc.; 55 (*Tyrannosaurus*): Marques/Shutterstock; 55 (*Cryolophosaurus*): Wikipedia; 57br: Louie Psihoyos/Corbis; 60–61: Francois Gohier/Photo Researchers, Inc.; 64–65: Millard H. Sharp/Photo Researchers, Inc.; 64bl, 64br: Black Hills Institute; 65tr: AP Photo/Randy Squires; 66tl, 66tr: Black Hills Institute; 66bl: Corbis; 66br: The Field Museum; 67tl, 67tr: Black Hills Institute; 67bl: National Geographic Stock; 67br: Craig Lovell/Corbis; 70tc, 70tr, 70bl, 70bc: Thinkstock; 73ct: Vladimir Sazonov/Shutterstock; 73cm: Tony Camacho/Photo Researchers, Inc.; 73cb, 73b: Thinkstock; 74–75 (timeline): Anton Prado Photo/Shutterstock; 74tl: Thinkstock; 74bl: Roblan/Shutterstock; 74bc: public domain; 74br: Natural History Museum, London/Photo Researchers, Inc.; 75tr: Thinkstock; 75c: Black Hills Institute; 75br: Viorika Prikhodko/iStockphoto.

### Artwork

1: Cary Wolinsky/Getty Images; 4–5 (background): MasPix/Alamy; 8tl: Francois Gohier/Photo Researchers, Inc.; 12 (tetrapod): Victor Habbick Visions/Photo Researchers, Inc.; 12 (*Coelophysis*): Natural History Museum, London/Science Photo Library/Photo Researchers, Inc.; 12–13 (Allosaurus): Roger Harris/Photo Researchers, Inc.; 17tr: Roger Harris/Photo Researchers, Inc.; 29tr: photobank.kiev.ua/Shutterstock; 34–35: Natural History Museum, London; 35bl: Christian Darkin/Photo Researchers, Inc.; 35br: Chris Howes/Wild Places Photography/Alamy; 36–37 (t background): MasPix/Alamy; 39t: Computer Earth/Shutterstock; 40–41: AlienCat/Bigstock; 41cr: Linda Bucklin/Shutterstc :; 51l: Walter Myers/Photo Researchers, Inc.; 58–59: Craig Chesek, copyright American Museum of Natural History; 62l: Roger Harris/Photo Researchers, Inc.; 62–63: DM7/Shutterstock; 63br: Roger Harris/Photo Researchers, Inc.; 65b: Tim Boyle/Getty; 68–69 (background): Christian Darkin/Photo Researchers, Inc.; 68bl: Ozja/Shutterstock; 69t: Christian Darkin/Photo Researchers, Inc.; 70tl: Thinkstock; 71: Julian Baum/Photo Researchers, Inc.; 73t: Ralf Juergen Kraft/Shutterstock; 77: Chris Howes/Wild Places Photography/Alamy; all other artwork: pixel-shack.com.

### Cover

Background: Baloncici/Crestock. Front cover: (tl) Handout/Reuters/Corbis; (c) Radius Images/Corbis; (bl) Phil Degginger/Alamy; (br) Friedrich Saurer/Photo Researchers, Inc. Spine: pixel-shack.com. Back cover: (tl) Corbis; (tcl) pixel-shack.com; (tcr) Dreamstime; (tr) pixel-shack.com; (computer monitor) Manaemedia/Dreamstime.